Contents

The Lion *and the* Mouse

The afternoon sun shone brightly on the plains. The mighty lion, king of beasts, strolled about in the tall grass. He was looking for a patch of shade in which to take a nap. At last he came to a spreading tree whose leaves dappled the ground with cool shadows. The lion lay down in the deepest part of the shade.

"Ah," he murmured, as he stretched himself in the soft dust. "What a nice place for a nap." He closed his eyes and began to snore gently.

After a time, a little mouse came scuttling past. She was in a hurry to reach her home, a tiny hole in the roots of the tree. In her haste, she didn't notice the sleeping lion until she had scampered right across his nose.

Of course, the tickle of four little mouse feet woke the lion instantly. He made one quick swipe and trapped the little mouse under his huge paw. Immediately she began to cry.

"Oh, please, Your Majesty, please don't kill me," she begged.

"Why not?" growled the lion. "You woke me from my nap."

"A thousand pardons," squeaked the mouse. "It was an accident. Besides, I have small mouse children to care for."

"That is none of my concern," muttered the lion. "Give me a better reason, or I shall flatten you."

"Well," answered the little mouse, trembling with fear, "if you spare me, I may someday be able to return the favor. I promise to help you in any way I can."

“Ha, ha!” laughed the lion. “I doubt you shall ever be able to help such a powerful one as myself. But you have amused me, so I shall let you go. Now run away quickly, and leave me in peace to finish my nap.”

With that, the lion raised his paw and set the mouse free. He chuckled to himself as he drifted off to sleep once more.

“How could a mouse ever help a lion? That will be the day.” Once again the lion’s gentle snores ruffled the afternoon air.

Several months later, the lion was once again out for an afternoon stroll. He was feeling rather haughty, and was not paying much attention to his surroundings. Suddenly he tripped over a rope that had been hidden in the grass. It was a trap! His paw was caught in a snare. As he struggled, a large rope net fell from a nearby tree. It covered the lion from head to toe. And the more he struggled, the more entangled he became.

This put the lion in a rage. He clawed and he scratched. He bit and fought. He threw back his royal head and roared in frustration.

Now luck would have it that the little mouse was nearby gathering seeds when the lion’s fearsome roar made the earth tremble at her feet. She picked up what seeds she could carry and made a dash for her safe little home. But after traveling only a few feet, she skidded to a stop. She listened. The roar came again.

"I had better go and see about this," she said to herself. "I have never heard the lion roar quite like that before. Something must be wrong!" Although she was quite frightened, she dashed toward the enormous sounds. In only a moment or two, she had reached the lion's side.

"Be still!" she shouted in her biggest voice. "All that roaring will bring the hunters down on us!"

"What difference does it make?" asked the lion. "I had just as well get it over with. I will never be free again." He threw back his head and roared again. This time he sounded more pitiful than fierce.

"If you will hush," insisted the mouse, "I shall have you out of here in no time."

To the lion's amazement, the mouse was already hard at work. He could hear the chomp, chomp, chomp of her sharp teeth and strong jaws. Soon she had bitten through several ropes. The lion pulled free of the net. He gazed gratefully at the little mouse.

"Thank you," said the king of beasts in a solemn voice. "You have proven to me that those who are small and weak may prove to be strong in friendship and kindness."

Questions about The Lion *and the* Mouse

A. 1. How did the lion feel about the mouse at the beginning of the story?

____

____

2. How did he feel about the mouse at the end of the story?

____

____

3. What happened to change the lion's feelings?

____

____

4. What lesson did the lion learn?

- ◯ Everyone should take a nap every day.
- ◯ Someone small and weak can be a good friend.
- ◯ Lions should only be friends with other lions.
- ◯ Getting angry is a good way to solve problems.

B. Think of a time when a friend has helped you. Write a short paragraph telling what happened and how you felt about it.

____

____

____

____

____

Tell It in Order

Number the following events in the order in which they occurred in the story. Place an **X** in front of any event that did not happen.

____ The mouse hears the lion roar.

____ The lion lies down in the shade to take a nap.

____ The lion catches the mouse.

____ The mouse chews the ropes.

____ The lion pulls free of the net.

____ The hunters run after the lion.

____ The mouse wakes the lion.

____ The lion gets caught in a trap.

____ The mouse makes a promise to the lion.

Fantastic Fact

A male lion can weigh up to 400 pounds (180 kilograms) and measure up to 10 feet (3 meters) in length.

What Does It Mean?

Fill in the circle in front of the choice that best replaces the underlined word or words.

1. Another word that means about the same thing as <u>mighty</u> is ________.

   ◯ strong ◯ powerful ◯ mean

2. In his <u>careless hurry</u>, Roger rushed out the back door and tripped over the dog.

   ◯ attention ◯ haste ◯ amazement

3. Some people <u>snore</u> when they sleep.

   ◯ dream ◯ talk ◯ breathe loudly

4. The lion was <u>amused</u> by the mouse's promise. He thought it was ________.

   ◯ funny ◯ scary ◯ rude

5. A <u>snare</u> is a kind of

   ◯ bird ◯ boat ◯ trap

6. The <u>enormous</u> stack of dirty dishes made me groan.

   ◯ large ◯ small ◯ huge

7. One <u>swipe</u> of the lion's paw would have been fatal to the little mouse.

   ◯ to steal ◯ to brush against ◯ to blow

8. The lion was <u>frustrated</u> because he could not break free from the trap.

   ◯ struggling to succeed ◯ prevented from carrying out a purpose

   ◯ ready to give up

Words for Sounds

A. Some words in the story imitate sounds. Use the "sound words" in the word box to complete these sentences.

Word Box					
murmur	squeak	growl	roar	chomp	hush

1. The dog might ____________________, but it won't bite.
2. "Susie, it is rude to ____________________ your gum that way," said Mr. Guthrie.
3. The crowd began to ____________________ when the rock band came onto the stage.
4. The baby's toy makes a little ____________________ when he squeezes it.
5. Robert was yelling at his sister, so his mother asked him to ____________.
6. Mrs. Larson's class began to ____________________ quietly among themselves when they heard the announcement.

B. Use the clues below to help you think of more sound words.

1. the sound of a bell ____
2. the cry of a kitten ____
3. the noise of a cannon ______________________________________
4. the sound of a fly ____
5. the noise of a car horn ______________________________________

Tricky Past Tense Verbs

A. Most verbs have the ending *ed* when they are in the past tense. But some verbs change entirely. These are called **irregular verbs.** An example of an irregular verb is *grow–grew.*

Write the past tense of each of these verbs.

1. begin ______________	11. go ______________
2. wake ______________	12. shoot ______________
3. catch ______________	13. forget ______________
4. bite ______________	14. know ______________
5. sleep ______________	15. think ______________
6. fly ______________	16. find ______________
7. fall ______________	17. feel ______________
8. lose ______________	18. speak ______________
9. build ______________	19. leave ______________
10. shake ______________	20. keep ______________

B. Use the past tense words above to fill in the blanks in this paragraph.

I ______________ a cold last week. It ______________ with a sore throat. I ______________ terrible. I ______________ to bed and ______________ for 16 hours. When I ______________ up, I sounded like a frog. I ______________ four pounds. I ______________ I would never get well, but now I am all better.

Character Traits

A. Write these words beneath the character they describe.

big	helpful	large	brave	strong	mother
kind	royal	tiny	scary	loyal	small
		sleepy	courageous		

Lion

______ ______
______ ______
______ ______

Mouse

______ ______
______ ______
______ ______
______ ______

B. In an **acrostic** poem, each line begins with a letter of the poem's subject. Read the acrostic about the lion in the story. Then write your own acrostic about the mouse.

lordly beast
in a terrible, roaring rage
out for an afternoon stroll he was
netted and held fast

m ______
o ______
u ______
s ______
e ______

An Oregon Trail Diary

This is a fictional account of the overland journey on the Oregon Trail. It is written in the form of a journal.

Sunday, January 30, 1852

We're going to Oregon! I heard Mother and Father talking late into the night last night. Father says that Oregon is beautiful, and all the land is rich and good. He says that we will prosper there. Mother doesn't seem so sure. She doesn't really want to leave our little farm here in Missouri. She has her chickens and turkeys and her milk cow and garden. Of course she won't be able to take them with us. I think she is a little bit sad. But I am excited! I heard Father say that we will travel in a covered wagon. Uncle Pleasant and Aunt Ellen are going too. That means that Cousin Amy will be with me! I can't wait to go.

Tuesday, February 16, 1852

It snowed this morning. All the trees look as if they have been dipped in sugar. It makes a pretty picture, but we are all hoping it will be the last snowfall of the season. We are eager for spring to come. We want to get started on our journey.

Saturday, March 16, 1852

The wagons are almost loaded. Today I helped Mother pack up all the things we will need to do our cooking along the trail. We packed everything in a wooden box that Father built. The front of the box folds down on hinges and makes a shelf where Mother can work. She calls the box our "camp kitchen." We put a Dutch oven and a large frying pan in the box. We also packed some wooden spoons, two sharp knives, and some tin plates and cups.

We have lots of food in the wagon. There are bags of dried apples and plums, sacks of beans and flour, and buckets of molasses. We have bacon and cured hams and some smoked fish. We have cornmeal and coffee and tea. We want to make sure that we have enough to eat on the journey.

Tuesday, April 12, 1852

Father has been very busy. He bought some oxen to pull the wagon. He has been gathering ropes, leather to repair harnesses, medicines for the animals, and who knows what all. He is taking tools like axes, shovels, and chisels. We will need many things when we get to Oregon, but we don't have room to carry very much. Father will use the tools to build us a house when we get there and to make beds and tables and chairs.

Mother is feeling happier about the trip. It has been hard work to get ready to go, but it is fun too. Just a few more days now!

Friday, April 15, 1852

Amy and I are going to sleep in the wagon tonight. And before daylight in the morning, we are leaving. I am going to bring my journal, but Father says I must choose just one toy to bring. It is very hard to decide, but I think I will bring Brenny, my rag doll. I love her most because Grandmother made her for me.

Monday, May 2, 1852

We are camped on the banks of the Missouri River. It is the biggest river I have ever seen. We cross tomorrow. At first I was afraid. But I have been watching the other wagons crossing on the flat ferryboats, and I think we will make it just fine.

It has been a good trip so far. The weather has mostly been sunny, which is lucky. The rainy days are hard to bear. We get so damp and cold, and it is hard to light a fire for cooking. The mud is very tiresome. It coats our shoes and splashes our stockings and aprons, and it is not easy to wash things. So we are glad for the sunshine. I had better go to sleep now. Tomorrow we cross to the west!

Tuesday, May 17, 1852

This prairie is so beautiful it takes my breath away. The grass is tall and waves in the wind. There are flowers everywhere. Amy and I picked our aprons full today as we walked. The only trees are near the river. We are camping for the night under the trees. The oxen are all drinking at the river now. Father is building a cooking fire. I will go and help Mother make something to eat. This is a glorious trip!

Goldenrod

Purple Clover

Pale Purple Cone Flower

Wednesday, June 29, 1852

We passed Independence Rock late this morning. This means we are making good time. It is important to make Independence Rock by the 4th of July, and we are nearly a week early! Immigrants always write their names on the rock. We all were eager to read the names, so we stopped to have something to eat and take a little rest. Father and Uncle Pleasant found the names of two friends who made the trip last year. Many of the people in our train added their own names to the rock.

After lunch we went a few more miles. We camped by the Sweetwater River. It is magnificent, with high cliffs on both sides. There is plenty of grass for the animals to eat. It is a lovely camp and I wish we could stay here a few days. But we have to keep moving. We still have a long way to go.

Sunday, July 17, 1852
Today we crossed some high mountains. They were covered with enormous pine trees that smelled wonderful in the hot sun. Even though the sun was very bright and hot, the air was cool and fresh. Amy and I found lots of wild berries. In camp some of the men caught some silvery trout from the stream that tumbled down the mountain. It was so nice to have fresh food for dinner.

Tuesday, August 9, 1852
The last few days have been very difficult. We had to cross a lot of country that is poor and dry. Some of the animals have died from sickness and want of water. Some of the people have been sick too, and everyone is very tired. We have not been able to rest much. We had to keep going so that we could get to a place where there is water. I think we will be all right now. Our camp here on the Burnt River is good. Some Indians came into camp with some large fish they wanted to trade. Mother gave them some corn bread and an old apron in trade for a fish, and we had a nice dinner.

Monday, September 5, 1852
These are mountains! The path we traveled today was steep and full of rocks. The men had to chop away fallen trees. As we go along, the way seems to get only steeper and higher. We are camped high up in these mountains with only a tiny stream for water. Aunt Ellen says she feels that we are on top of the world. It is hard going, and quite cold as evening comes on.

Thursday, September 8, 1852

We came down from the mountains today. The trail plowed straight down the mountain. The oxen were slipping and sliding. The heavy wagons pressed on them. All the men had to help hold the wagons back. The trail was so narrow and steep that we feared the wagons would pitch right over the side. All of us children had to stay away from the trail because it was so dangerous. We had to find our own way down the hill, and it was a hard job because there were huge boulders and fallen logs strewn over every inch of the mountainside. I am still shivering with fright and tiredness.

Monday, October 3, 1852

Another adventure. We sailed the Columbia River today. The Indians took us in their canoes. It was rainy and blustery all day. The waves were wild and kept splashing over the sides. Amy was terrified, but for some reason I quite enjoyed the excitement. Perhaps it is because our journey is nearly at an end.

Sunday, October 16, 1852

This is a day to give thanks. Father and Mother have found the land for our new home. Our family will claim 640 acres. We are camping on the land tonight. Father says he will start to work on a cabin right away, but we will have to stay with some other settlers for the winter months. Our land is wonderful. There is a spring of sweet water and there is deep grass, and the soil is dark and good. The air smells like mint. We are full of joy.

Questions about
An Oregon Trail Diary

1. Father wanted to go to Oregon ______.
   - ◯ to get some good, rich land
   - ◯ to get a job in a factory
   - ◯ because his friends lived there
   - ◯ because Mother wanted to go

2. How did Mother feel?

____

____

3. How did the girl who wrote the diary feel?

____

____

____

4. The journey had both pleasant and unpleasant experiences. Tell about two of each.

____

____

____

____

Tell It in Order

Fill in the circle next to the correct answer.

1. Did the family load the wagons before or after February 16?

○ before ○ after

2. Did they pass Independence Rock before or after the Fourth of July?

○ before ○ after

3. Did they travel in Indian canoes before or after they crossed the mountains?

○ before ○ after

4. Did the girls pick flowers before or after they picked berries?

○ before ○ after

5. Did they buy fish from the Indians before or after Father bought some oxen?

○ before ○ after

6. Was Father planning to make furniture before or after they arrived in Oregon?

○ before ○ after

Fantastic Fact

One of the first things pioneers did when they got to their new homes was to buy land. The price of land was about $2.00 an acre. This was a lot of money for many pioneers.

What Does It Mean?

Write the words below in the correct columns.

Foods	People	Feelings

fright	uncle	flour	joy
father	mother	bacon	excitement
terrified	corn bread	fish	cousin
apples	molasses	glad	plums
beans	Amy	gloomy	grandmother

Understanding What You Read

Fill in the circle next to the correct answer.

1. The family traveled to Oregon in ______.

   Ⓐ a small plane
   Ⓑ a covered wagon
   Ⓒ a pick-up truck
   Ⓓ a passenger train

2. What did the family take to eat on the journey?

   Ⓐ beans
   Ⓑ bacon
   Ⓒ dried apples
   Ⓓ all of the above

3. While the girls were in the mountains, they picked some ______.

   Ⓐ berries
   Ⓑ flowers
   Ⓒ walnuts
   Ⓓ tomatoes

4. Items used for cooking were stored in ______.

   Ⓐ a canvas sack
   Ⓑ a tin can
   Ⓒ a wooden box
   Ⓓ a plastic crate

5. Which toy did the little girl decide to take with her on the journey?

   Ⓐ jump rope
   Ⓑ checker set
   Ⓒ rag doll
   Ⓓ yo-yo

6. It was important for the family to camp in a grassy area at night because ______.

   Ⓐ grass is nice to sit on
   Ⓑ their animals needed grass to eat
   Ⓒ the children wanted to play ball
   Ⓓ looking at the pretty grass made them feel happy

Compound Words

Combine each word from List A with a word from List B to create compound words. Write the compound words on the lines below.

A	B
every	boat
day	light
grand	top
sun	meal
corn	house
ferry	mother
fish	where
rain	shine
farm	fall
mountain	hook

The Journey to Oregon

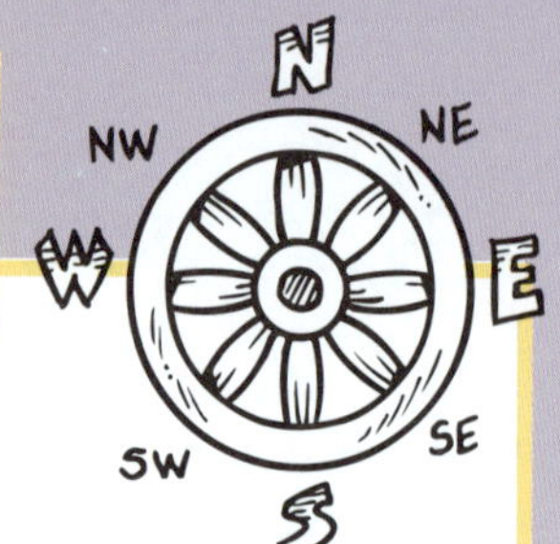

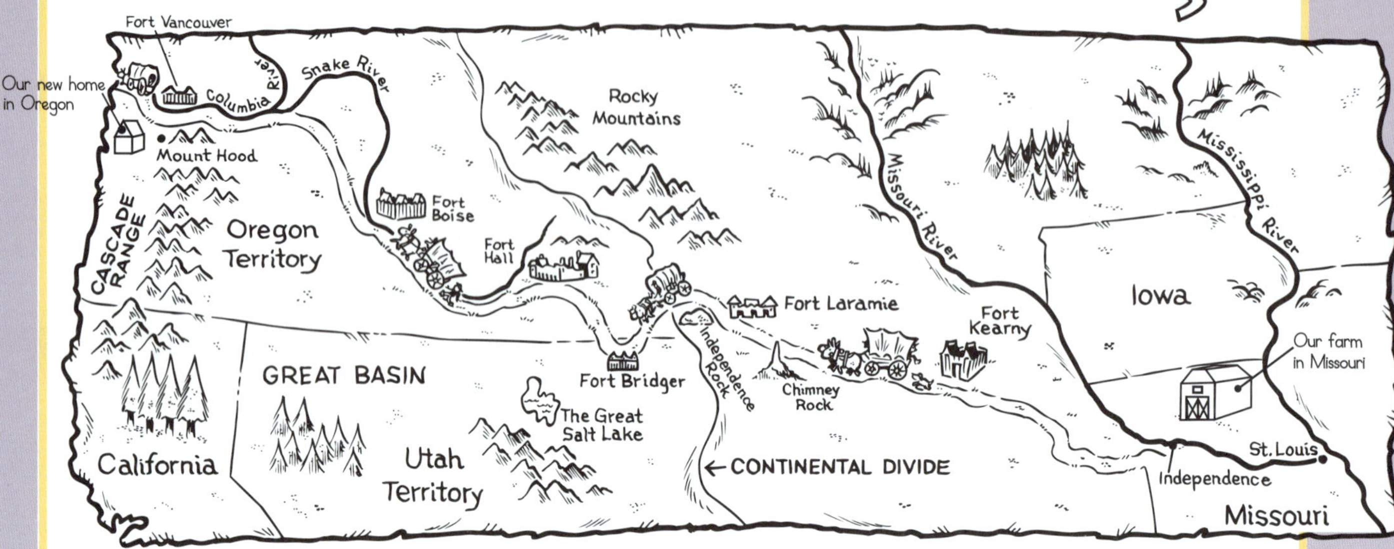

Fill in the circle next to the correct answer.

1. The Oregon Trail passed to the ________ of the Great Salt Lake.
   - Ⓐ north
   - Ⓑ south
   - Ⓒ east
   - Ⓓ west

2. Which is the first fort the family would have come to on their journey?
   - Ⓐ Fort Bridger
   - Ⓑ Fort Hall
   - Ⓒ Fort Boise
   - Ⓓ Fort Kearny

3. The Rocky Mountains are to the ________ of the Cascade Mountains.
   - Ⓐ north
   - Ⓑ south
   - Ⓒ east
   - Ⓓ west

4. Which river forms the eastern boundary of Missouri?
   - Ⓐ Mississippi
   - Ⓑ Columbia
   - Ⓒ Missouri
   - Ⓓ Snake

How to Make a Pair of Stilts

Have you ever tried to walk on stilts? It's harder than it looks, but it is lots of fun. It is a good way to improve your balancing skills. Ask a parent or an adult to help you make a pair of stilts.

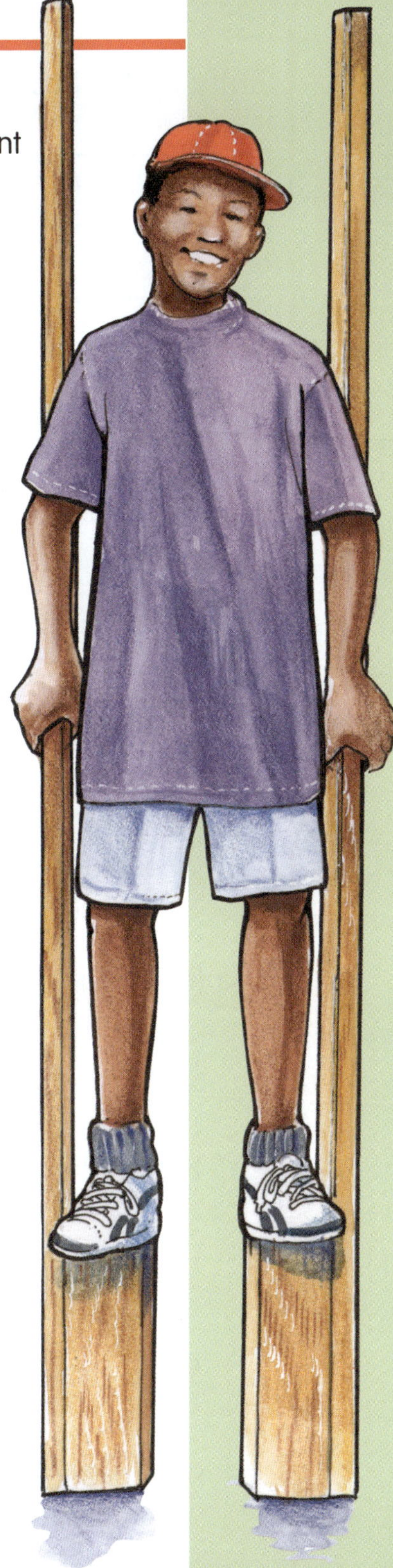

You will need:

- a tape measure
- a saw
- wood glue
- a hammer
- nails
- handles—2 6′ (1.8 m) lengths of 1″ x 2″ (2.5 x 5 cm) lumber
- steps—2 10″ (25.5 cm) lengths of 2″ x 4″ (5 x 10 cm) lumber
- sandpaper
- paint (optional)

Make the handles

1. Ask your helper to measure the distance from the ground to the top of your shoulders. Add 1 foot to this measurement.
2. Cut each piece of the 1″ x 2″ lumber to this measurement.
3. Sand these handles carefully. You want to make sure there are no splinters!

Add the steps

1. Spread wood glue on one long side of each 2″ x 4″ piece of lumber.
2. Attach these steps to the bottom of the handles. Make sure that the bottom of the handle is even with the bottom of the step.
3. Use the hammer to drive four nails through each handle and into the step.
4. If you like, paint your stilts to make them more colorful and fun to look at.

Tips for walking on stilts

1. Practice standing on the stilts first. Ask your helper to steady the stilts until you feel comfortable on your own.
2. Hold the handles of the stilts so they are behind your arms.
3. Use the handle of each stilt to pull the step up against your foot as you walk.
4. Be patient. Keep trying. As your skill improves, you can make new stilts with taller steps.

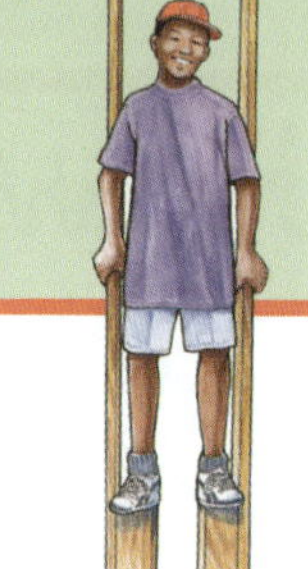

Reading a Graph

Stilts are fun because they make you tall.

Use the information in the graph to answer these questions about some tall things!

How tall is the giraffe?

How tall is the building?

Which is taller, the tree or the building?

Which is taller, the giraffe or the flagpole?

Ask someone to help you measure yourself to see how tall you are.

I am

What's the Opposite?

A. Write the number of each word on the line in front of its antonym.

1. tall	____ sour
2. happy	____ rough
3. push	____ miserable
4. smooth	____ over
5. under	____ calm
6. rise	____ tiny
7. cool	____ pull
8. enormous	____ heavy
9. asleep	____ short
10. sweet	____ fall
11. excited	____ warm
12. light	____ awake

B. Draw two pictures in each box to illustrate the pair of opposites given.

even uneven

smooth rough

The Old Woman Who Lived in a Vinegar Jug

Once, long ago in merry old England, a magic bluebird was flitting about in the woods. She heard a noise and followed it to a small clearing. There, between the trees, was a large vinegar jug. Outside the jug there was a little old woman. She was pacing back and forth in front of the vinegar jug.

When the old woman saw the bluebird, she began to grumble.

"Woe is me. Woe is me. It's ever so unfair. Why must I live in a vinegar jug? I should live in a sweet little cottage with a fireplace and windows and flowers by the door. Woe is me. Woe is me."

The kindhearted bluebird took pity on the little old woman.

"All right," said the bluebird. "Just snap your fingers three times and see what happens." With that, the bluebird disappeared.

The old woman snapped her fingers three times. She climbed into her rough, little bed and went to sleep. When she awoke in the morning, she found herself in a pretty bedroom. Sunlight streamed through the windows. A fire crackled in the fireplace. Outside, flowers bloomed by the door. She was very excited, but she thought no more of the little bluebird.

Time passed and a year rolled away. The magic bluebird decided to go see the little old woman. She wanted to see the happiness her gift had brought. When the bluebird arrived, she was surprised to find the little old woman pacing back and forth in front of the cottage.

When the old woman saw the bluebird, she began to grumble.

"Woe is me. Woe is me. It's ever so unfair. Why must I live in a simple cottage? I should live in a two-story house with fine furniture and china dishes. Woe is me. Woe is me."

The bluebird was a little hurt that the old woman didn't even bother to say thank you. But as you will remember, she was a kindhearted creature.

"Oh well," thought the bluebird. "She has never had nice things. It is not so much to ask."

"All right," said the bluebird. "Just snap your fingers three times and see what happens." And with that, the bluebird disappeared.

The old woman snapped her fingers three times. She climbed into her pretty bed and went to sleep. When she awoke in the morning, she was in an elegant bedroom. She ran down the stairs and saw a gleaming table set with china dishes. She was very excited, but she thought no more of the little bluebird.

Time passed and another year rolled away. The magic bluebird decided to go see the little old woman. She wanted to see the happiness her gift had brought. When the bluebird arrived, she was amazed to find the little old woman pacing back and forth in front of the two-story house.

When the old woman saw the bluebird, she began to grumble.

"Woe is me. Woe is me. It's ever so unfair. Why must I live in a mere house? I should live in a mansion with long hallways and many rooms. Woe is me. Woe is me."

The bluebird was a bit upset that the old woman didn't even bother to say thank you. But as you will remember, she was a kindhearted creature.

"Oh well," thought the bluebird. "She has never had wealth. It is not so much to ask."

"All right," said the bluebird. "Just snap your fingers three times and see what happens." And with that, the bluebird disappeared.

The old woman snapped her fingers three times. She climbed into her elegant bed and went to sleep. When she awoke in the morning, she was in an ornate bedroom. She spent the whole day exploring the many lovely rooms. She was very excited, but she thought no more of the little bluebird.

Time passed and yet another year rolled away. The magic bluebird decided to go and see the little old woman. She wanted to see the happiness her gift had brought. When the bluebird arrived, she was astonished to find the little old woman pacing back and forth in front of the mansion.

When the old woman saw the bluebird, she began to grumble.

"Woe is me. Woe is me. It's ever so unfair. Why must I live in a regular mansion? I should live in a castle with servants and silver and gold. Woe is me. Woe is me."

The bluebird was quite annoyed that the old woman didn't even bother to say thank you. But as you will remember, she was a kindhearted creature.

"Oh well," thought the bluebird. "She has never had power. It is not so much to ask."

"All right," said the bluebird. "Just snap your fingers three times and see what happens." And with that, the bluebird disappeared.

The old woman snapped her fingers three times. She climbed into her ornate bed and went to sleep. When she awoke in the morning, she was in a golden bed. Two servants helped her dress in a gown of velvet and silk. Another servant brought her a lavish breakfast on a silver tray. Gardeners worked among beds of beautiful roses. The old woman was very excited, but she thought no more of the little bluebird.

Time passed and again a year rolled away. The magic bluebird decided to go and see the little old woman. She wanted to see the happiness her gift had brought. When the bluebird arrived, she was flabbergasted to find the little old woman pacing back and forth, forth and back, in front of the castle.

When the old woman saw the bluebird, she began to grumble.

"Woe is me. Woe is me. It's ever so unfair. Why must I live in a regular castle? I should live in a fabulous palace and be queen of all the world. Woe is me. Woe is me."

The bluebird was extremely annoyed that the old woman didn't even bother to say thank you. And even though she was a kindhearted creature, she was completely out of patience.

"Well, well," thought the bluebird. "This has gone entirely too far."

"All right," said the bluebird. "Just snap your fingers three times and see what happens."

The old woman did not notice the bluebird's grouchy tone. She was already thinking about how delightful it would be to be queen of all the world. She snapped her fingers three times. She climbed into her golden bed and went to sleep. When she awoke in the morning, she was back in her vinegar jug, where some say she deserved to be all along.

And she never saw the magic bluebird again.

After You Read

Practice reading aloud the colored section on this page. Read the old woman's words to show that she felt unhappy and dissatisfied. Read the bluebird's words to show that it was annoyed.

Questions about

The Old Woman Who Lived in a Vinegar Jug

Decide whether each statement is probably true or probably false. Explain why you think so, giving examples from the story.

1. The old woman who lived in the vinegar jug had a cheerful personality.

   This statement is probably ____________ because ____________________

   ____.

2. The magic bluebird enjoyed making people happy.

   This statement is probably ____________ because ____________________

   ____

   ____.

3. The old woman was grateful for the gifts she received.

   This statement is probably ____________ because ____________________

   ____.

4. If she had become queen of the world, the old woman would have been happy.

   This statement is probably ____________ because ____________________

   ____.

5. At the end of the story, the old woman got what she deserved.

   This statement is probably ____________ because ____________________

   ____.

Tell It in Order

In the story the old woman lived in several different houses. In the boxes below, draw a picture of each of these houses in the order in which they appeared in the story. Label each picture. The first one has been done for you.

1. vinegar jug

2. ______________________

3. ______________________

4. ______________________

5. ______________________

6. ______________________

What Does It Mean?

Use the words in the word box to complete the sentences.

Word Box

amazed	annoyed	flabbergasted
ornate	astonished	elegant
grumbled	flitted	grouchy
lavish	jug	mere

1. The ______________ chair was covered with fancy decorations.
2. We were ______________________ to learn that we had won first prize.
3. Matt was ________________ with his sister because she grabbed the book out of his hand.
4. Ellen was ______________________ when her kitten began to fly.
5. The dainty horse pranced in a graceful and ________________ manner.
6. Silas ___________________ about having too much homework to do.
7. The butterfly ______________ from flower to flower.
8. The __________________ carpenter complained all day.
9. Jean gave Carol a ___________________ gift of diamond jewelry.
10. Kim poured the maple syrup out of the ____________________.
11. Sam was paid a ______________________ dollar for all his hard work.
12. Lynn was ________________________ when her friends gave her a surprise birthday party.

Alphabetical Order

A. Here is a list of things the old woman wanted. Write them in alphabetical order.

fireplace ______________________

windows ______________________

silver ______________________

furniture ______________________

rooms ______________________

servants ______________________

dishes ______________________

hallways ______________________

flowers ______________________

gold ______________________

B. Imagine the home you would most like to live in. Make a list of five things you would find in that home. Then write your list in alphabetical order.

List	List in Alphabetical Order
1. ______________	______________
2. ______________	______________
3. ______________	______________
4. ______________	______________
5. ______________	______________

Suffixes

A **suffix** is a word part that is added to the end of a base (root) word. Suffixes can change the meaning of the base word.

The suffix ***ness*** means "a state of being."

The suffix ***less*** means "without."

The suffix ***ful*** means "full of."

The suffix ***er*** means "a person who."

Add a suffix to each of the words below. Then write the meaning of the new word on the line. For words ending in *y*, you may have to change the *y* to an *i* before adding the suffix.

		Meaning of the word with the suffix
good	__________	____________________
care	__________	____________________
thought	__________	____________________
complain	__________	____________________
beauty	__________	____________________
hope	__________	____________________
grumble	__________	____________________
kind	__________	____________________
happy	__________	____________________
worth	__________	____________________

Understanding What You Read

Fill in the circle next to the correct answer.

1. The bluebird instructed the old woman to _____.

   Ⓐ click her heels together two times
   Ⓑ count to ten
   Ⓒ snap her fingers three times
   Ⓓ clap her hands five times

2. The bluebird went to visit the old woman after ______ had passed.

   Ⓐ one week
   Ⓑ one year
   Ⓒ one day
   Ⓓ one month

3. The bluebird gave the old woman all of these kinds of houses except _____.

   Ⓐ a cottage
   Ⓑ a mansion
   Ⓒ a castle
   Ⓓ a palace

4. The bluebird was upset because the old woman did not say _____.

   Ⓐ hello
   Ⓑ thank you
   Ⓒ good night
   Ⓓ good-bye

5. The old woman was ______.

   Ⓐ greedy
   Ⓑ cheerful
   Ⓒ unselfish
   Ⓓ thoughtful

Dick Whittington

and His

Wonderful Cat

Hundreds and hundreds of years ago in England there lived a simple orphan boy named Dick Whittington. Both of his parents had died. He was completely and totally alone. He had no relatives to care for him.

For a time, Dick tried to manage the farm that was left to him, but he was not old enough or strong enough. The fences broke down and the animals ran away to find food. The garden grew choked with weeds. There was not a bite of food to eat.

One day Dick decided that he had better go to London. There he would look for some kind of a job. So he set off walking down the road. He knew London was a great distance away. He wasn't sure he would ever get there, but he didn't know what else to do. Hour after hour, he bravely trudged along. Late in the day he stopped to make a little camp for himself under a tree. Another traveler was already there. He was a thin man with grizzled hair. He seemed a rough character, but he spoke pleasantly. He offered Dick some bread from his knapsack.

"So you're on your way to London, are you?" asked the man.

"Yes, sir," replied Dick. "I must go to the city to find a job and make my way in the world."

"Oh, you'll like London," said the man, smiling. "It is a marvelous city. There are tall buildings and fancy people. Some say the streets are paved with gold! One more day's walk and you will be there."

Dick's head was full of dreams that night. In his dreams he wandered the streets of a wonderful city, picking golden coins from between the cobblestones. When he awoke in the morning, he was on his feet in a flash. He bid his companion good-bye and fairly danced down the road.

The sun was setting when Dick reached the outskirts of the city. He fell to his knees and began to scrape at the pavement. He hoped to see the shine of gold. All he found for his trouble was cold stone covered with dirt. He was very hungry. He asked the people in the street where a willing boy might find work. The people pushed him away without listening. They were not interested in the questions of a ragged, dirty boy.

Dick was discouraged, cold, and tired. He found a doorway in an alley out of the wind. He curled up and cried himself to sleep. Sometime later, Dick awoke with a start. The sky was becoming dark. He heard the thump of large boots approaching over the cobblestones. He sat up, his heart racing.

A large shape carrying a lantern appeared out of the gloom.

"Ho! What's this?" boomed a loud voice.

The lantern was pushed close to Dick's face. Frightened, he scooted deeper into the doorway. "Don't be scared, lad," said the big voice. "I'm not going to hurt you."

The voice belonged to the merchant whose doorway Dick had chosen for his nap. The man took a closer look at the shivering boy.

"You look hungry, child, and you have an honest face. Let me take you to the kitchen. Cook will get you something to eat and a pallet to sleep on. Tomorrow you can begin working for me. I need an errand boy. What do you say?"

Dick was overcome with joy.

"Oh, thank you, sir!" he said. "I gratefully accept your offer."

So the merchant showed Dick into a big kitchen. A fire blazed in a huge stone fireplace. Cook was a large woman with a gruff manner but kind eyes. She gave Dick a bowl of soup and a mug of fresh milk. Then she showed him to a little straw bed in the pantry. Dick sank happily into a sound sleep.

Dick liked his job as errand boy for the merchant. When he was not busy at the merchant's office or warehouse, he helped Cook with kitchen chores. One day Dick sat on the kitchen doorstep peeling potatoes. He felt a nudge at his elbow. He was surprised to see a little white cat with bright yellow eyes gazing at him and purring.

"Why, aren't you a dear!" cried Dick. "Cook, come here and see!"

Cook came running. They both fussed over the kitten. Cook brought a saucer of milk and a kipper on a plate. The cat ate every morsel. Then she sat down beside Dick and licked her paws. From that time on, the cat stayed quite close to Dick. She followed at his heels as he went about his errands. She chased down every mouse that dared to show its whiskers in the kitchen. Cook was delighted.

Dick also took the cat with him to the merchant's warehouse. She quickly got rid of the wharf rats that ran in and out among the bales and boxes. The merchant was delighted.

Although Dick dreamed of making a better life for himself someday, he was happy so long as his little white cat was near. After a year or two had passed, the merchant came to Dick.

"One of my trading ships is sailing soon," said the merchant. "I need your help with a problem."

"Of course," said Dick. "Anything at all. How can I help?"

"Well, you see," answered the merchant, "this ship is overrun with rats. The captain is beside himself. Your cat is the best mouser I have ever seen. Will you let her go on this voyage?"

"You know I would do anything for you, sir," said Dick sadly. "But I cannot sell my cat. She is all the world to me."

"You would not have to sell her," replied the merchant. "Just rent her to me for this voyage. In a few months she'll be back safe and sound. I shall pay you half a crown for her rent."

Dick was not happy about being parted from his pet. But he did not want to disappoint the merchant, so he agreed.

He took the cat down to the dock and put her on the ship. She set right to work catching rats. Dick stood forlornly on the shore and waved until the ship was out of sight.

The weeks turned into months. Dick grew very lonely for his little cat. He began to wonder if she would ever come back. Finally, when the ship had been gone for nearly a year, Dick began to give up hope. One day, filled with sadness, Dick packed his few clothes into a bundle and set off into the countryside.

"I can no longer stay here without my little cat," he thought woefully. "I cannot bear the memories. I had better go back to the farm."

Nearly blinded by tears, he stumbled out of the city. He sat down on a stone beside the road and wept, pouring out his grief.

While he sat, the bells from a nearby church began to chime. As they rang they sang a special song that seemed to be meant for his ears alone:

Turn again, Dick Whittington,
Turn again, again.
Turn again, Dick Whittington,
And be Lord Mayor of London.

Dick thought he must be daft, but the bells pealed their message over and over again. At last he said to himself, "Daft or not, I had better heed this message."

Feeling strangely full of hope, Dick trotted back into London. As he neared the merchant's warehouse, he saw a flurry of activity. A ship was in the harbor. Men were scurrying to unload it. It was the merchant's ship, come safely home. With a burst of joy, he ran as fast as he could. When he reached the dock, there was his little cat, bounding up to greet him. It was a joyous reunion. Dick rushed home with the little cat. He and Cook spent several hours petting the animal and feeding it every kind of treat imaginable.

Late in the day, the merchant appeared in the kitchen.

"Here you are, Dick," chuckled the merchant. "Here is your payment for renting the cat."

He held out a gold coin, which Dick took gleefully.

"Thank you, sir," he laughed. "But it is payment enough to have my little cat at home again."

"Not so," said the merchant. "In fact, I have quite a surprise for you. Let me tell you something of your cat's adventures. It seems that our captain sailed into a faraway port in a rich land. The king of that land invited him to supper in his splendid castle. When they sat down to eat, rats came scrambling from every corner of the room. They leaped onto the tables and gobbled up the food. It was terrible! The captain asked the king how he could bear such misery. The king replied that he did not know how to solve the problem. The captain promised to solve the problem and do it quickly. The next day he put your little cat into a sack and brought it into the castle. He set her free to do her work. He told the king he would be back to pick her up on his return voyage. When he returned, the castle was free of rats. The delighted king insisted on giving the captain a handsome reward. The captain has sent part of the reward to you."

With that, the door opened and a burly sailor came into the kitchen. He was toting a heavy wooden chest. He plunked it on the floor and left without saying a word. The merchant and Cook drew close to Dick.

"Open it!" they cried.

The little cat rubbed against his leg and looked at him expectantly. Her eyes twinkled at him. He felt sure she was smiling.

With trembling hands, Dick threw back the lid of the chest. Inside were pearls, rubies, gold coins and chains, beautiful silks, and rare spices. An amazing array of riches spilled from the rough container.

"My boy, you are rich!" exalted the merchant. "How would you like to be my partner?"

So Dick Whittington became a London merchant. Before too many years passed, he was one of the wealthiest men in the city. Finally, in his mature years, loved and respected by all, Dick Whittington became Lord Mayor of London. And he owed it all to his little white cat.

Questions about Dick Whittington *and His* Wonderful Cat

Write a sentence or two explaining what happened to solve each of these problems from the story.

1. Dick was left alone on the family farm.

____

____

____

2. When Dick got to London he was cold and hungry and had to sleep in a doorway.

____

____

____

3. The merchant's ship was full of rats.

____

____

____

4. Dick feared his cat was gone forever. He was heartbroken.

____

____

____

5. Dick was very poor.

____

____

____

Tell It in Order

A. List the following story characters in the order in which they appeared.

people on the London streets
a thin man with grizzled hair
the cook
a burly sailor
the merchant
the cat
Dick Whittington

1. ______________________________
2. ______________________________
3. ______________________________
4. ______________________________
5. ______________________________
6. ______________________________
7. ______________________________

B. Dick decided to leave London because he was so lonely for his cat. What did he hear that made him turn around and go back to the city?

◯ a bird singing
◯ a dog barking
◯ church bells ringing
◯ the beating of a drum

What Does It Mean?

Draw lines to match each word to its definition.

cobblestones	rough or rude
lantern	large bundles
gruff	round stones used to pave a street
errand	to carry
chore	an impressive display
burly	a trip to deliver a message or do a particular thing
wharf	a lamp that can be carried
bales	a dock
daft	a businessman
merchant	a small job
tote	crazy
array	strong

Contractions

A. Write the contraction for each set of words.

1. you have ______________
2. I am ______________
3. do not ______________
4. is not ______________
5. can not ______________
6. it is ______________
7. she will ______________
8. they are ______________

B. Write the two words that form each contraction.

1. aren't ______________
2. haven't ______________
3. wouldn't ______________
4. we're ______________
5. they'll ______________
6. who's ______________
7. hasn't ______________
8. I've ______________

C. Write two sentences. In each sentence you must use two contractions.
For example: *If you **haven't** finished your chores, you **won't** get to play ball with your friends.*

1. ____

____

____

2. ____

____

____

Understanding What You Read

Fill in the circle next to the correct answer.

1. Dick went to London because ______.

   Ⓐ he could no longer take care of his farm
   Ⓑ his parents wanted to move there
   Ⓒ he wanted to become a firefighter
   Ⓓ his grandmother took him there

2. Dick's little cat had ______.

   Ⓐ black fur and green eyes
   Ⓑ gray fur and blue eyes
   Ⓒ orange fur and brown eyes
   Ⓓ white fur and yellow eyes

3. Dick Whittington grew up to be a ______ man.

   Ⓐ good
   Ⓑ bad
   Ⓒ lazy
   Ⓓ cruel

4. Cook gave Dick ______.

   Ⓐ an apple and a piece of cheese
   Ⓑ a sausage and a pickle
   Ⓒ a bowl of soup and a mug of milk
   Ⓓ a sandwich and a cookie

5. The ship's captain loaned the cat to ______.

   Ⓐ a child
   Ⓑ a king
   Ⓒ a teacher
   Ⓓ a sailor

6. What hardship did Dick experience in his life?

   Ⓐ loneliness
   Ⓑ loss of parents
   Ⓒ hunger
   Ⓓ all of the above

Analogies

An **analogy** is made up of two pairs of words that have a similar relationship.

Up is to ***down*** as ***small*** is to ***large***.

The first pair of words, *up* and *down*, have opposite meanings, so the second pair must also have opposite meanings.

Complete each analogy.

1. *Cat* is to *animal* as *banana* is to ____________________.
2. *Dirty* is to *clean* as *cold* is to ____________________.
3. *Walk* is to *run* as *smile* is to ____________________.
4. *Stream* is to *river* as *alley* is to ____________________.
5. *Hat* is to *head* as *boot* is to ____________________.
6. *Bread* is to *eat* as *water* is to ____________________.
7. *Eye* is to *see* as *ear* is to ____________________.
8. *Fur* is to *cat* as *feather* is to ____________________.
9. *Card* is to *deck* as *page* is to ____________________.
10. *Milk* is to *cow* as *egg* is to ____________________.

Challenge:

Make up some analogies of your own. Get your family and friends involved.

____

____

____

Go Fly a Kite

A kite catches the wind. Tugging at the string, it pulls upward, dipping and swaying. The string unwinds. The kite climbs higher and higher into the blue. Its colorful shape looks beautiful against the sky. Flying a kite is a fun way to spend a spring day.

People around the world have been flying kites for centuries. In fact, kites were invented over two thousand years ago! One ancient story tells of a Chinese general named Han Hsin. He was in charge of a small army. The army was trying to overthrow a cruel emperor. Han Hsin built a kite. He had his soldiers fly it in the direction of the palace. When the kite was over the palace, Han Hsin marked the string. He reeled in the kite.

Then he measured the string from his mark to the kite. He used this measurement to plan a tunnel to the palace. His soldiers crept through the tunnel. They popped up inside the walls of the palace. The cruel emperor was defeated with the help of a simple kite!

Kites have also been used in modern warfare. Before airplanes were invented, cameras were tied to kites. They were sent high in the air to take pictures. This was a way of gathering information about enemy forces.

Kites have also been used to carry radio equipment up into the air. This made the signals easier to send and receive. In World War II, kites were used as targets for shooting practice. Kites were also included as part of the emergency kit in lifeboats. People stranded in the lifeboats could fly the kites. Searchers would see the kites and come to their rescue.

Kites have been used in many other ways. People have used kites to carry instruments high into the clouds. There the instruments measured temperature and wind speed. Sometimes the kites could not fly high enough. When this happened, they were sometimes tied together in trains. First one kite was sent sailing on a long string. This string was tied to a second kite. This kite helped to lift the first kite even higher. A third and even a fourth kite might be added to the train.

One famous event involving a kite was Benjamin Franklin's experiment. Franklin wanted to show that lightning was a form of electricity. He thought that if he sent a kite up into the clouds he could find out for sure. Franklin made his kite carefully. He used two lightweight sticks. He covered the sticks with a square of silk fabric. He attached an iron wire to the frame of the kite. Then he attached a long string. Near the end of this string, Franklin tied a brass key. Then Franklin tied a piece of silk ribbon to the end of the string. He would use this ribbon to hold onto the kite. He knew that silk would not conduct electricity very well. He hoped it would keep him safe.

On a stormy afternoon, Franklin set out to try his kite. A brisk breeze was blowing. Franklin's kite rose quickly into the dark clouds. Raindrops were pelting down. As a safety measure, Franklin stood in the doorway of a barn. Water is a good conductor of electricity. He knew he needed to keep the silk ribbon dry. Franklin reached out and tapped the key with his finger. Sparks flew! It was electricity!

Franklin was happy with the success of his experiment. He was also very lucky. He could have been badly injured or even killed. It is very important to remember that you should *never* fly a kite on a stormy day. Metal should never be used in the making of a kite. Also, kites should never be flown around power lines.

Today, kites are used mostly for fun. Families go to open spaces like parks or beaches to fly kites. Sometimes there are even kite-flying contests.

In China there is a special holiday for kites. It is called Kites' Day. There is a legend that is told on Kites' Day. The legend says that long, long ago a man in China had a dream. He dreamed that his house and family would be destroyed on the ninth day of the ninth month. On that day he took his family up in the hills. Together they flew kites all day. When they returned home, they found their house had tumbled down. There was nothing left but a pile of rubble. But the family was safe.

Now, on the ninth day of the ninth month, many Chinese people go outside and fly kites. The kites are made to look like brightly colored birds, graceful butterflies, or even enormous dragons. They hope that the flying of the kites will bring good luck.

In Japan special kites are flown on May 5. This holiday was first called Boys' Day. On this day families would fly kites to celebrate the birth of baby boys during the past year. Each family also flew windsocks. Windsocks are a kind of kite. They were flown on a tall bamboo pole. There was a windsock for each boy in the family. Each windsock was shaped like a carp. The carp is a fish that is very strong. It can swim against a strong current. The carp was a symbol of the hard work and courage needed to succeed in life. Today, girls are included in the celebration. The name of the holiday has been changed to Children's Day. Kites and windsocks are still part of the fun.

Kites can be large and elaborate, or small and simple. Many kites are very inexpensive. You can even make a kite of your own, using nothing more than sticks, paper, tape, and a ball of string. So the next time you are looking for something fun to do, go fly a kite!

Box Kite

Chinese Kite

Japanese Carp Windsock

How to

Make a Kite

Gather these materials:

- two strips of balsa wood; one 24″ (61 cm) long, one 36″ (91.5 cm) long
- wood glue
- string
- brown wrapping paper—36″ (91.5 cm) wide roll
- craft knife
- crayons or marking pens (optional)
- strips of lightweight cloth

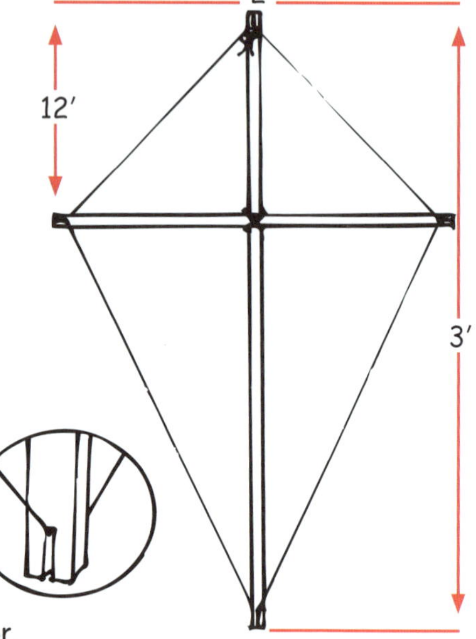

Make the kite frame

1. Ask an adult to help you cut a narrow slit in both ends of the balsa strips.
2. Lay the shorter strip across the longer one. Secure with glue.
3. Tie this joint with string and allow the glue to dry.
4. Tie a string to one end of a strip.
5. Run the string through the slits on all the ends of the strips, forming the outline of your kite.
6. Cut the string.

Put the covering on the kite

1. Spread wrapping paper on the floor. Lay your kite on the paper.
2. Cut the paper 1″ (2.5 cm) larger than your kite on all sides.
3. Decorate the kite if you wish.
4. Fold the edges of the paper over the strings and glue.

Make a bridle for your kite

1. Cut a piece of string 48″ (1 m 22 cm) long.
2. Tie the string to the top and bottom of the lengthwise stick on the front side of the kite. Leave some slack. (See colored kite at top.)

Make a tail for your kite

1. Tie another string to the bottom of the vertical stick. This string should be 3′ to 4′ (1 to 1.22 m) long.
2. Tie some strips of lightweight cloth to the string.

Tie a ball of string to the bridle at about the place where the sticks cross.

Questions about
Go Fly a Kite

1. Name three ways people have used kites.

____

____

____

2. Why did Benjamin Franklin fly a kite?

____

____

3. You should never fly a kite ______ .

○ on a hill ○ during a storm

○ in the morning ○ by yourself

4. Why is Kites' Day celebrated in China?

____

____

____

5. The windsocks flown in Japan on Children's Day are shaped like what animal? Why?

____

____

____

Tell It in Order

Write a paragraph explaining the steps in building a kite.
Include these words: *first, next, then, after that, finally.*

Fantastic Fact

The American Kitefliers Association has over 4,000 members in 35 countries. A calendar of kite festivals can be found on this Web site: http://www.aka.kite.org

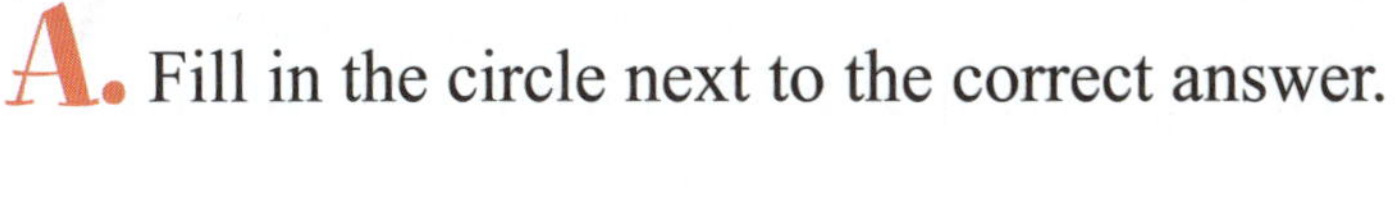

What Does It Mean?

A. Fill in the circle next to the correct answer.

1. What does an *emperor* do?
   - ◯ design a building
   - ◯ drive a tractor
   - ◯ rule a country

2. An *emergency* is
   - ◯ an ambulance
   - ◯ an urgent situation that must be taken care of right away
   - ◯ a first-aid kit

3. *Electricity* is
   - ◯ a form of energy
   - ◯ a light switch
   - ◯ happiness

4. When you do an *experiment* you
   - ◯ must ask a friend to help
   - ◯ conduct a test
   - ◯ work in a lab

5. *Equipment* is
   - ◯ a kind of horse
   - ◯ a joke
   - ◯ the tools and supplies you need to do a job

B. Match each word with a word that means the opposite.

enemy	cheap
elaborate	small
enormous	friend
expensive	simple

In the Dictionary

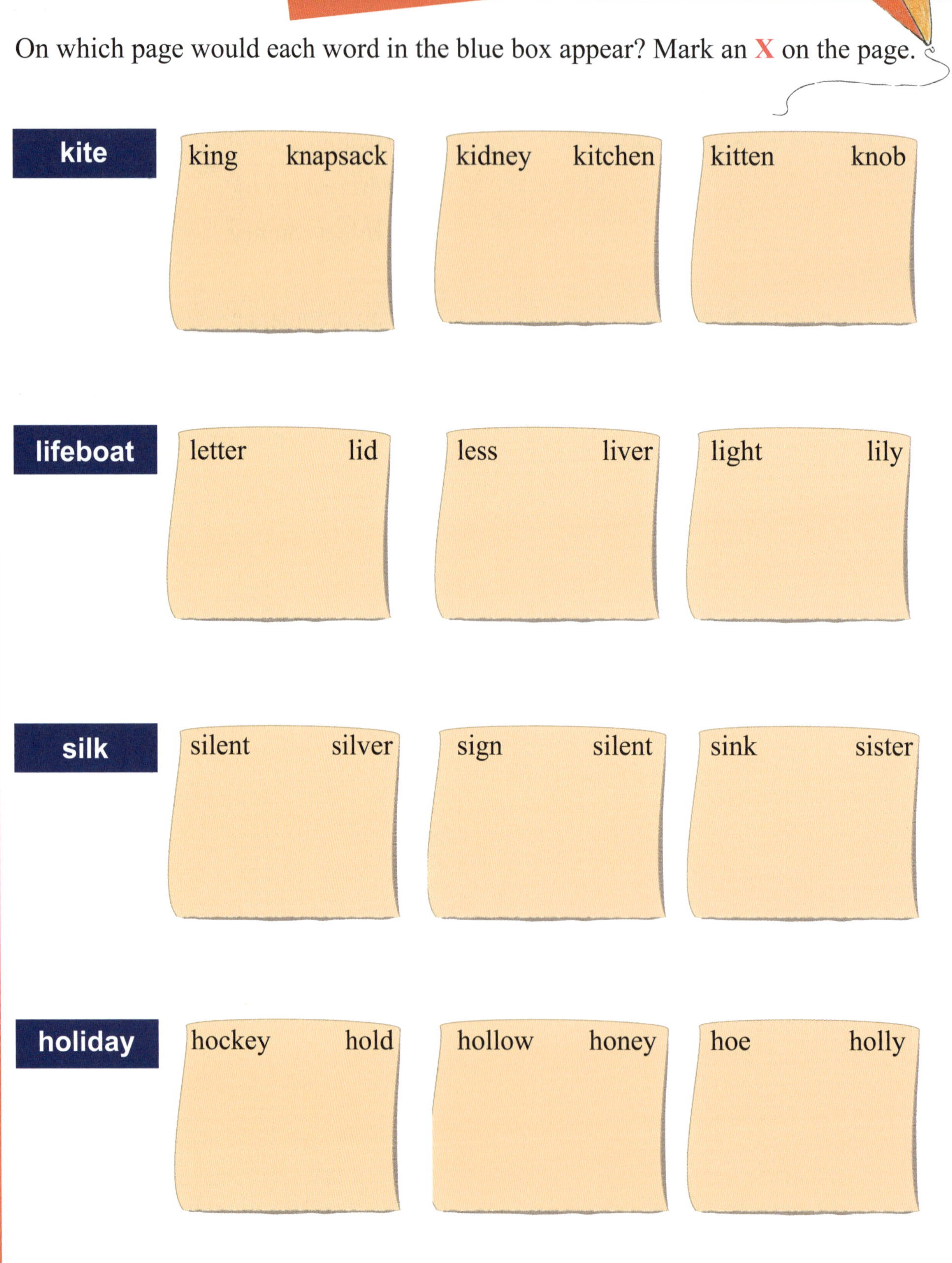

On which page would each word in the blue box appear? Mark an X on the page.

Word	Page 1	Page 2	Page 3
kite	king — knapsack	kidney — kitchen	kitten — knob
lifeboat	letter — lid	less — liver	light — lily
silk	silent — silver	sign — silent	sink — sister
holiday	hockey — hold	hollow — honey	hoe — holly

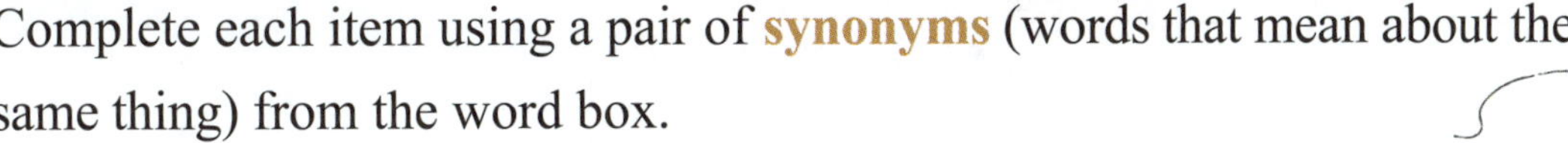

Synonyms

Complete each item using a pair of **synonyms** (words that mean about the same thing) from the word box.

Word Box

mean	courage	contest	wind
legend	powerful	ancient	fall
show	breeze	rescue	story
old	tumble	demonstrate	strong
bravery	save	cruel	competition

1. ____________________ means about the same as ____________________.
2. ____________________ means about the same as ____________________.
3. ____________________ means about the same as ____________________.
4. ____________________ means about the same as ____________________.
5. ____________________ means about the same as ____________________.
6. ____________________ means about the same as ____________________.
7. ____________________ means about the same as ____________________.
8. ____________________ means about the same as ____________________.
9. ____________________ means about the same as ____________________.
10. ____________________ means about the same as ____________________.

Fantastic Fact

Other famous kite fliers besides Ben Franklin include the Wright brothers, inventors of the first "flying machine," and Alexander Graham Bell, inventor of the telephone.

Whose Kite Is Whose?

Find out which kite each child is flying.

Use the clues given. Mark the grid boxes with an **X** when you know that a person **does not** have a particular kite. When you have only one unmarked box in a row, write ***Yes*** in that box.

Lee, Lynn, Jade, and Erika are all flying kites.

Lee's kite is not blue.

Jade's kite is not flying as high as Erika's.

Erika's kite is flying higher than the red kite.

The yellow kite does not belong to Lynn.

Lee's kite is not shaped like a butterfly.

Lynn's kite is flying lower than the blue kite.

Erika's kite is not yellow.

The highest-flying kite is the butterfly.

	blue	yellow	red	butterfly
Lee				
Lynn				
Jade				
Erika				

Let's Go to the Movies

Super Cinema
3804 Broadway Ave.
555-1616

All seats
$3.00
until 5 o'clock!

Now Playing

Theater 1

Lost in the Galaxy	12:30	3:15	8:00
Ice Mountain	1:00	4:00	7:00
Knights of the Round Table	12:45	3:00	6:30
Cyclone	1:15	4:15	7:15

Theater 2

Voyage to Beyond	2:00	4:30	7:00
Mitzi & Mittens: Two Kittens	12:00	3:10	6:30
The Wild Horses	1:45	4:00	6:15
Danny's Dinosaurs	12:15	2:45	5:45

Theater 3

Adventure Express	2:30	4:30	7:20
King of the World	1:20	3:45	6:10
Ballet Story	1:30	4:10	6:50
Blueberry Summer	2:00	5:30	7:30

Questions about Let's Go to the Movies

1. Betsy and Hilda want to see a movie that starts after 7:15. Which movie should they choose?

   ◯ The Wild Horses ◯ King of the World

   ◯ Lost in the Galaxy ◯ Danny's Dinosaurs

2. How many showings of *Danny's Dinosaurs* will be screened today at the discount price?

   ____

3. Which movie will be screened only once at the discount price?

   ____

4. Judging from the titles…

   which movies are probably outer space adventures? ______________________________

   ____

   which movie is probably about a dancer? ______________________________

   which movies probably feature animal actors? ______________________________

   ____

5. Which one movie listed would you pick to see?

   ____

   What is something that might happen in this movie? ______________________________

   ____

   ____

Alphabetical Order

Write these movie titles in alphabetical order. *Hint:* A title that begins with the word "The" is alphabetized by the next word in the title.

Lost in the Galaxy ____________________

Ice Mountain ____________________

Knights of the Round Table ____________________

Voyage to Beyond ____________________

Mitzi & Mittens: Two Kittens ____________________

The Wild Horses ____________________

Danny's Dinosaurs ____________________

King of the World ____________________

Ballet Story ____________________

Blueberry Summer ____________________

Capitals in Titles

Six new movies will open at the Super Cinema next week. Rewrite the movie titles using capital letters where they belong.

the best fourth of july ever ____________________

rocky the rowdy raccoon ____________________

the prince and the pauper ____________________

the man who looked in the mirror ____________________

the magic unicorn ____________________

destination mars ____________________

The Three Sillies

A farmer and his wife lived in a small farmhouse on a neat little farm. They had a daughter with dark curly hair. This daughter had a sweetheart. The sweetheart was a gentleman of considerable education and wealth.

The gentleman often came to the farmhouse to have dinner with his sweetheart's family. When he came, the daughter always brought him a glass of cider from the keg in the cellar. One evening the daughter was just setting plates and cutlery on the table when she heard hoofbeats in the yard. Then came a knock at the door. The farmer opened the door to find the gentleman on his doorstep.

"Good evening!" said the gentleman.

"Please come in," said the farmer, "and welcome, indeed."

The gentleman took off his dusty hat and seated himself in his usual comfortable chair. The daughter greeted him cheerfully and skipped off to the cellar to get a glass of cool cider.

She turned the tap on the cider barrel and held the glass beneath it. The amber liquid began to trickle into the glass. The girl looked about the cellar as she waited for the glass to fill. On glancing up, her eyes lit upon a rusty ax stuck fast in a beam above her head. Strange thoughts began to fill her head.

"What if I should marry my sweetheart and have a lovely son. And what if that son should grow up to be a fine young man. And what if that fine young man should come down to this cellar to fetch his sweetheart a glass of cider. And what if that ax should fall on his head, 'Ka-whump!' That would be the end of him. How absolutely terrible, how utterly unbearable, that would be!"

Completely forgetting about the cider, she sat down on a bench and began to sob and wail. The cider trickled on, making a puddle on the cellar floor. Soon the farmer came down the steps. When he saw his daughter sitting by the puddle of cider, his eyes grew wide.

"Whatever is the trouble, my dear?" he asked.

Still sobbing, the girl pointed to the rusty ax stuck in the beam above her head.

"Oh, Father. What if I should marry my sweetheart and have a lovely son. And what if that son should grow up to be a fine young man. And what if that fine young man should come down to this cellar to fetch his sweetheart a glass of cider. And what if that ax should fall on his head, 'Ka-whump!' That would be the end of him! How absolutely terrible, how utterly unbearable, that would be!"

The farmer was overcome by the thought. He sat down on the bench beside his daughter. He too began to sob and wail. The cider trickled on, making a stream on the cellar floor.

Soon the farmer's wife came down the steps. When she saw her husband and daughter sitting by the stream of cider, her eyes grew wide.

"Whatever is the trouble, my dears?"

Still sobbing, the girl pointed at the rusty ax stuck in the beam above their heads.

"Oh, Mother. What if I should marry my sweetheart and have a lovely son. And what if that son should grow up to be a fine young man. And what if that fine young man should come down to this cellar to fetch his sweetheart a glass of cider. And what if that ax should fall on his head, 'Ka-whump!' That would be the end of him! How absolutely terrible, how utterly unbearable, that would be!"

The farmer's wife was overcome by the thought. She sat down on the bench next to her husband. She too began to sob and wail. The cider trickled on, making a river on the cellar floor.

Now, the gentleman was waiting all this time for his cider. He was becoming quite thirsty so he too came down the steps. When he saw the whole family sitting on a bench beside the river of cider, his eyes grew wide. He quickly turned off the bubbling cider tap.

"What on earth is the trouble here?" he exclaimed.

Still sobbing, the girl pointed at the rusty ax stuck in the beam above their heads.

"What if you and I should marry and have a lovely son. And what if that son should grow up to be a fine young man. And what if that fine young man should come down to this cellar to fetch his sweetheart a glass of cider. And what if that ax should fall on his head, 'Ka-whump!' That would be the end of him! How absolutely terrible, how utterly unbearable, that would be!"

All three began wailing and sobbing anew.

But the gentleman began to laugh uncontrollably.

"Why you are nothing but supreme sillies!" he sputtered. He reached up for the ax handle, and with a jerk removed it from the beam and brought it safely down to his side. "I do not think I wish to marry into such a silly family. I will go and travel the wide countryside, and if I find three anywhere who are sillier than you, I shall return."

The gentleman mounted his handsome horse and rode rapidly away from the farm. After a week or so of traveling, the gentleman came to a cabin with a sod roof. Grass grew from the sod, and a wooden ladder leaned against the side of cabin. An old lady was there, trying to push a spotted cow up the ladder.

"What in the world are you doing?" asked the gentleman.

"Why, I'm putting my cow on the roof to eat grass," replied the old woman. "Isn't it obvious?"

She pushed and shoved and tugged until at last the cow stood upon the roof. "Now I shall drop her rope through the chimney and tie it to my wrist. Then I shall be able to do my work and not have to worry about my cow."

And that is what she did. No sooner had she knotted the rope around her wrist than the spotted cow tumbled off the edge of the roof. The old lady shot up the chimney where she wedged tight. The gentleman cut the rope, freed the cow, and pulled the old lady out of the sooty chimney.

"My, my," he thought as he rode away. "There is the *first* silly I came to seek."

A week or two later, the gentleman rode up to a country inn. It was late in the evening, and all the rooms were already taken. The innkeeper told him that he could share a room with another traveler. The gentleman agreed to this arrangement, because he was quite tired. He climbed the stairs to his room, got into one of the beds, and went right to sleep. When he awoke in the morning his roommate was already up. He was a short, stout fellow. He was holding his pants out in front of him. He made a mighty hop and leaped at his trousers. One leg slid in and there he stood, one leg in his trousers and one leg out. He withdrew the leg and tried again. Over and over he hopped and he jumped, trying to leap into his pants.

The gentleman could hardly contain his laughter.

"Let me show you an easier way," said he.

The gentleman pulled on his pants in the normal way, one leg at a time, and left the room, shaking his head.

"My, my," he thought as he rode away from the inn. "There is the *second* silly I came to seek."

A week or two later, he rode into a rustic village. There was a lovely millpond in the center of the village. As it was a warm day, the gentleman rode up to the pond to give his horse a drink. There by the side of the pond was a young man with a net, which he cast into the water.

"Are you fishing for trout?" asked the gentleman, with interest.

"Oh no, sir," the young man replied. "I am trying to net the moon. You see, I saw it here in this very pond last night, and I'm trying to pull it out!"

The gentleman had to bite his lip to keep from laughing out loud.

"Wait 'til nightfall," said the gentleman, "and all will be well."

The young man looked at him doubtfully, and threw his net once more into the pond.

"My, my," thought the gentleman as he rode away from the village. "There is the *third* silly I came to seek."

And so he turned his horse around and trotted back toward the farm where his silly sweetheart and her silly family waited for him. The two were married, and we may hope they lived happily together for a long, long time.

After You Read

Find a part of this story that you think is really silly and funny. Practice reading it aloud until your reading is smooth. Read it to someone. Did you make them laugh?

Questions about The Three Sillies

1. Why did the daughter go down to the cellar?

   ◯ to fetch some cider ◯ to put wood on the fire

   ◯ to hide some jewels ◯ to take a nap

2. What did she see when she looked above her head?

   ____

3. Why did the gentleman go down to the cellar?

   ____

   ____

4. Explain how the daughter's imagination caused a problem.

   ____

   ____

   ____

5. Who solved the problem? How?

   ____

   ____

6. Pretend that the gentleman met a fourth silly in his travels. Tell what that silly did.

   ____

   ____

   ____

   ____

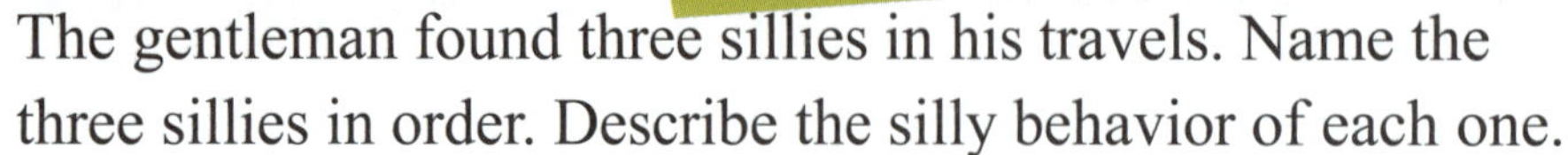

Tell It in Order

The gentleman found three sillies in his travels. Name the three sillies in order. Describe the silly behavior of each one.

First silly: ____________________

____

____

____

____

Second silly: ____________________

____

____

____

____

Third silly: ____________________

____

____

____

____

What Does It Mean?

Find the word in the story that matches each meaning below.

1. a sweet drink often made from apples ________________
2. a basement ________________
3. a small barrel ________________
4. a structure that lets smoke escape from a fireplace ________________
5. a small, rough house ________________
6. a tool for chopping ________________
7. a hotel in the country ________________
8. a fine black powder left over from burning ________________
9. table utensils; silverware ________________
10. grass with dirt attached ________________
11. a name for a loved one ________________
12. a slow drip or stream of liquid ________________
13. crying uncontrollably ________________
14. almost impossible to withstand ________________
15. a man with good manners ________________

Understanding What You Read

Fill in the circle next to the correct answer.

1. The family of sillies lived in ______.

   Ⓐ a castle

   Ⓑ a cave

   Ⓒ a hut

   Ⓓ a farmhouse

2. The traveler at the inn did not know how to ______.

   Ⓐ put on his shirt

   Ⓑ put on his pants

   Ⓒ get out of bed

   Ⓓ eat breakfast

3. At the end of the story, the gentleman went ______.

   Ⓐ to the city and got a job

   Ⓑ to the beach and went swimming

   Ⓒ back to the farm and married his sweetheart

   Ⓓ to the market to buy some bread

4. Why did the old lady want to put her cow on the roof?

   Ⓐ to frighten birds

   Ⓑ to rest in the sun

   Ⓒ to eat the grass

   Ⓓ none of the above

5. The young man with the net was trying to ______.

   Ⓐ catch a fish

   Ⓑ catch a frog

   Ⓒ pull his friend out of the pond

   Ⓓ pull the moon out of the pond

"More" and "Most"

The suffix ***er*** means "more." It is used when comparing **two things**.

*This pencil is long**er** than that pencil.*

The suffix ***est*** means "most." It is used when comparing **three or more things**.

*Of all the pencils, this one is the long**est**.*

A. Add the correct suffix to each word below. Notice that all the words end in ***y***. Remember to change the ***y*** to an ***i*** before adding the suffix.

1. more happy ______________________
2. most silly ______________________
3. more easy ______________________
4. more rusty ______________________
5. most wealthy ______________________
6. more pretty ______________________
7. most sleepy ______________________
8. most funny ______________________

B. Write sentences using ***er*** and ***est*** correctly.

1. Compare the height of two boys. ______________________

____

2. Compare the speed of four cars. ______________________

____

3. Compare the temperature yesterday and today. ______________________

____

Silly Sentences

Change one word in each silly sentence to create a new sentence that makes sense.

1. Angie went for a ride on her new desk.

____

2. Mrs. Anderson told the children to write sentences using their spelling bananas.

____

____

3. Dad put soup in Marie's shoe.

____

4. Jan planted some alligator seeds in her garden.

____

5. We paddled our canoes down the street.

____

6. Manuel kicked the pretzel across the goal line.

____

Penguins, Pelicans, and Puffins

Penguins, pelicans, and puffins are all birds. They live in and around the oceans of the world. Each of these seabirds has an interesting or unusual feature.

Penguins

Penguins are famous for their handsome black-and-white coats and the funny way they waddle. Penguins are unusual birds because they cannot fly. They are terrific swimmers, however, and spend a great deal of time in the water. They use their wings to paddle in the water. They have webbed feet that help them swim. Their bodies are coated with a thick layer of waterproof feathers. The fat on their bodies helps to keep them warm even in icy water.

A penguin begins life as an egg. Both parents help to care for the egg. They keep it warm until it hatches. It takes nearly a whole day for the chick to break out of the egg. When the chick does come out, it needs a lot of protection. The parents must keep it warm and bring it food to eat. They must also keep the chick safe from predators. One parent hunts for food while the other parent watches the chick. As the chick grows bigger, it needs more and more food. Both parents must return to the sea to find enough to feed the hungry baby. When this happens, the chick is hidden among the rocks. Many parents may hide their babies together. When the young penguin is big enough, it joins its parents in the sea, learning to swim and hunt for its own food.

A dangerous time for the young penguin comes when it begins making trips into the sea on its own. The penguin must stay alert for predators.

There are seventeen different kinds of penguins in the world. Some penguins are quite large. Emperor penguins are the largest. These penguins grow to about four feet tall and weigh up to one hundred pounds. Emperor penguins have an unusual way of hatching eggs. The female lays an egg on the ice. The male rolls the egg up on top of his feet. He covers the egg with his fat belly and keeps it warm until it hatches.

The smallest penguins are the little blue penguins. Sometimes they are called "fairy penguins." They are only about ten inches tall. They live on the coasts of Australia and New Zealand.

© Digital Stock

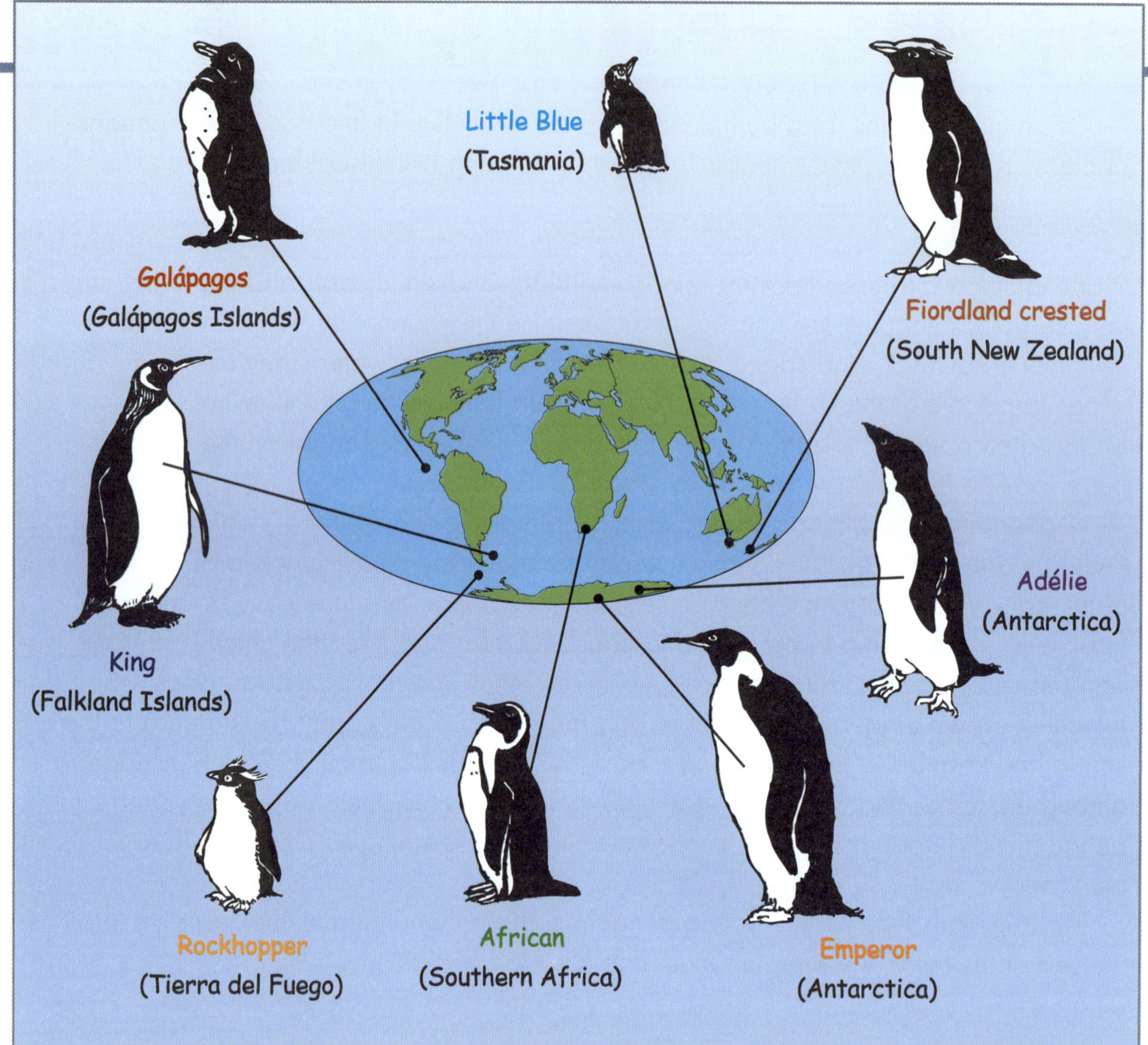

Penguins live in the Southern Hemisphere. This map shows some of the areas where penguins make their homes.

Adult penguins shed their feathers each year. This is called "the molt." During the molt, the penguins' feathers fall out. New feathers grow in. The penguins cannot go into the water until their new feathers grow in. They have to wait onshore. They probably get cold and hungry. They need the new feathers to keep them warm and protected for another year.

Adélie penguins are what most people picture in their mind when they think of penguins. They are striking in their black-and-white "suits." They build nests out of stones and lay two eggs at a time.

Chinstrap penguins have a band of black feathers beneath their chin that looks like the chinstrap of a hat or helmet. These penguins have a loud, shrill cry. People claim this piercing cry is loud enough to break stones! So these penguins are sometimes called "stonecrackers."

Pelicans

Pelicans are fascinating birds with an odd appearance. They are large and awkward-looking birds. They don't move around much on land. They can fly and they are good swimmers.

© David Bridge

Pelicans have a large pouch attached to the bottom part of their bills. They use this pouch to scoop up fish. They may take in two or three gallons of water as well. They push the water out of the pouch and then swallow the fish whole. Pelicans eat as much as four pounds of fish every day.

Pelicans live mostly along the coasts of oceans and on the shores of some large lakes. They are quite social and often flock together. Brown pelicans, also known as American pelicans, nest together in large colonies. They build nests in bushes, trees, or even on the ground. The nests are built of sticks, grass, and straw. Two eggs are laid in the spring. The eggs hatch in about one month. Parents feed and protect the babies until they are old enough to manage on their own.

Brown pelicans have very good eyesight. They use this ability to help them find food. They fly over the ocean searching for fish. When they see a fish they dive into the water and scoop it up.

© Digital Stock

Brown pelicans weigh about ten pounds and have a wingspan of about seven feet.

Brown pelicans were nearly made extinct. Fishermen thought that pelicans were eating too many fish. They killed many adult pelicans and destroyed their eggs and nests. At the same time, pesticides like DDT were killing the pelicans. In1970 pelicans were placed on the list of endangered species. Studies were done to show fishermen that pelicans were eating fish that people don't like to eat. In 1972 DDT was banned in the United States. Slowly the pelicans began to recover. In some areas of the country, pelicans are no longer endangered.

Puffins

Puffins are cute. Their stout, little black-and-white bodies are topped off with round heads that sport large, brightly colored beaks. Puffins live on the shores of the cold North Atlantic Ocean and nearby seas.

Puffins eat fish. Their large beaks are specially made for catching and holding large numbers of small fish. There are rows of little hooks inside their beaks that help them hold onto their slippery catch.

Some people think that puffins are flying penguins, but this is not true. Puffins do look a bit like penguins. They have similar coloring. They are also good swimmers and like cold water. But puffins live in the Northern Hemisphere. Penguins live in the Southern Hemisphere. They are two different kinds of birds.

Puffins group together in large flocks. They spend most of their time in the water. Sometimes they gather on the rocky shoreline. They like a roaring wind because it helps them fly. Puffins often fly in large groups. Thousands of puffins will take to the skies, flying in a large circular pattern.

Puffins build nests on grassy slopes or under rocks. In the summer each breeding female lays one egg. When the baby puffin hatches, the parents take turns bringing food until the young one is ready to leave the nest. In Iceland people have a special way to help the puffins who live on their shores. In August of each year, thousands of baby puffins called "pufflings" leave their nests and try to fly. This first effort at independence is made at night when predators are sleeping. But many of the pufflings get confused. They fly to the city instead of the sea. In the city there are many dangers. The pufflings might be run over by cars or chased by dogs. Even if they survive these dangers, they will surely starve. The people of the city, especially the children, all join the hunt. They search all over the city for pufflings. They return them to the shore. In this way thousands of puffins each year are given a new chance at life.

Puffins are curious birds that take a great interest in one another.

After You Read

When you read nonfiction articles, you often have to pronounce names of places and special terms. Read the last paragraph aloud. Practice until you are sure you can read it correctly and clearly. Then read it aloud to someone.

Questions about
Penguins, Pelicans, and Puffins

Write a ***T*** in front of each statement that is true. Write an ***F*** in front of each statement that is false.

1. _____ Penguins are mammals.
2. _____ Puffins live in large flocks.
3. _____ Penguins are good swimmers.
4. _____ Pelicans cannot fly.
5. _____ Penguins eat fruit.
6. _____ Penguins hatch from eggs.
7. _____ There are twelve different kinds of penguins.
8. _____ Pelicans eat fish.
9. _____ Pelicans have poor eyesight.
10. _____ Puffins cannot fly.
11. _____ Baby puffins are called "pufflings."
12. _____ Pelicans have pouches under their bills.

Fantastic Fact

A father Emperor penguin loses about half his weight (30 pounds or 15 kilograms) while waiting for the baby to hatch.

Tell It in Order

Write these sentences in order. Leave out any sentence that does not belong.

Then he covers the egg with the fat on his belly.

Emperor penguins have an unusual way of hatching chicks.

The parents bring food to the chick.

After a while, the chick hatches out of the egg.

The mother penguin lays an egg on the ice.

Pelicans dive into the water to catch fish.

When it is big enough, the chick learns to swim and find food.

The father penguin rolls the egg on top of his feet.

____

____

____

____

____

____

____

____

____

____

What Does It Mean?

A. Match each word to its definition.

awkward	thick or chubby
survive	having died out completely
stout	half of the Earth
hemisphere	to lose feathers
molt	to live
predator	clumsy
scoop	joined together by skin
extinct	an animal that catches other animals for food
pouch	a bag or sack
webbed	to gather in, as with a bucket

B. Use words from the list above to fill in the blanks.

All penguins live in the Southern ____________________ . With their _______________ bodies they appear _______________ on land. In the water, however, they are adept and graceful swimmers. Their _______________ feet and stiff wings are used to propel them through the water. Penguins have learned to _______________ in an environment that most animal species would find difficult if not impossible to live in.

Spell It Right!

A. Circle the correct spelling for each word.

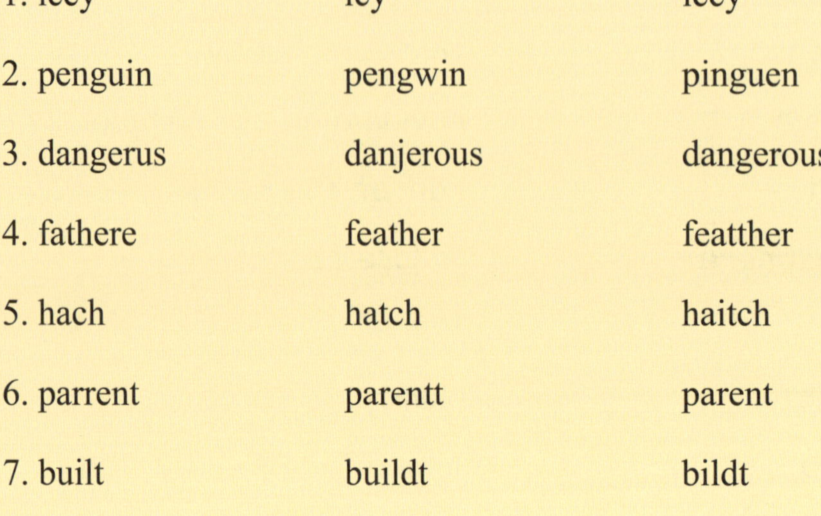

1. icey	icy	iccy
2. penguin	pengwin	pinguen
3. dangerus	danjerous	dangerous
4. fathere	feather	featther
5. hach	hatch	haitch
6. parrent	parentt	parent
7. built	buildt	bildt
8. enuff	enough	enouf
9. proteck	proteckt	protect
10. famous	famouse	faimous

B. Write sentences using the correct spellings of the words in numbers 3, 7, and 8 above.

1. ____

____

2. ____

____

3. ____

____

Write It Right!

Write each sentence correctly. Consider capitalization, punctuation, and grammar.

1. lets go to the zoo said lucy

____

2. will we be able to see the penguins asked jim

____

3. the zoo is on orange street

____

4. you isnt allowed to pet the animals

____

5. there are lions tigers jaguars and cheetahs at the zoo

____

____

6. andy and mother likes the elephants

____

7. Six bears was swimming in the pool

____

8. dad bought hot dogs for lucy and i

____

Understanding What You Read

Fill in the circle next to the correct answer.

1. Which kind of penguin is the largest?
   - Ⓐ Emperor
   - Ⓑ King
   - Ⓒ African
   - Ⓓ Rockhopper

2. Brown pelicans have a wingspan of about ______.
   - Ⓐ 2 feet
   - Ⓑ 4 feet
   - Ⓒ 7 feet
   - Ⓓ 10 feet

3. Puffins like a strong wind because wind ______.
   - Ⓐ blows insects away
   - Ⓑ helps the puffins fly
   - Ⓒ keeps the puffins cool
   - Ⓓ sweeps litter off the beach

4. Penguins build their nests out of ______.
   - Ⓐ ice
   - Ⓑ grass
   - Ⓒ stones
   - Ⓓ sticks

5. Brown pelicans live in large groups called ______.
   - Ⓐ colonies
   - Ⓑ apartments
   - Ⓒ communities
   - Ⓓ crowds

6. What do children in Iceland do to help the puffins?
   - Ⓐ They take baby puffins home to be pets.
   - Ⓑ They take lost baby puffins back to the shore.
   - Ⓒ They take puffins to the zoo.
   - Ⓓ They take puffins to the veterinarian.

Blindfold Treasure Hunt

This is a funny game to play with your family.

You will need:

- a blindfold
- a stopwatch, watch with a second hand, or kitchen timer
- five small household objects such as a sponge, a ball, a shoe, a plastic cup, and so on. Choose items that are not sharp or breakable.
- a cardboard box or paper bag

What to do

1. Place the objects in a line at one end of a fairly large indoor or outdoor space.
2. Set the box or bag about ten feet away.
3. The person who is "it" sits by the box and puts on a blindfold.
4. He or she must crawl on hands and knees and find one of the objects, then crawl back to the box and place the object in the box. This must be repeated until all items have been collected.
5. Each player takes a turn being "it." The player who completes the job in the shortest time wins.

Questions about Blindfold Treasure Hunt

1. Would members of your family enjoy playing this game? Why or why not?

2. What are the names of the people you would like to play this game with?

3. What objects that you have at home would you choose to be the "treasure"?

4. What would you use for a blindfold?

5. Do you think this would be an easy game or a hard game? Why?

Fantastic Fact

For over 200 years, treasure hunters have been looking for buried treasure on Oak Island in Mahone Bay in Nova Scotia, Canada.

Put It Where It Belongs

In the word box below are a number of household items that could be used in a "Blindfold Treasure Hunt." Divide them into three groups and then name each group.

Word Box

sock	pot lid	ring
jump rope	catcher's mitt	tennis ball
spoon	scarf	ice cube tray
sunglasses	measuring cup	plastic food container
Ping-Pong paddle	glove	bicycle helmet

________	________	________
Name of Group	Name of Group	Name of Group
________	________	________
________	________	________
________	________	________
________	________	________
________	________	________

Leprechauns

Leprechauns are magical folk of Irish legend. They are little old men about two feet in height. Leprechauns are said to wear green clothing and leather aprons. They wear funny little hats. Their shoes are decorated with buckles.

Most leprechauns are not very friendly. They usually stay away from people. However, leprechauns have been known to do helpful things for people on occasion. Most often this will occur at night and in secret.

Leprechauns are said to be shoemakers. According to the legends, they make shoes for elves and fairies. If you want to find a leprechaun, you must listen closely for the sound of a tiny hammer tapping away on a tiny shoe.

Leprechauns have lucky charms. Any small item given to a person by a leprechaun will bring good luck. Leprechauns are quite wealthy. Each leprechaun has a pot of gold that is well hidden. Some say each pot of gold is hidden at the end of a rainbow. Anyone who catches a leprechaun may demand the pot of gold, and the leprechaun must tell where it is hidden.

But as you will learn in the following story, this is not quite as simple as it seems. For leprechauns are very tricky.

Catching a Leprechaun

Irish words in the story:

Breda (Bree´ dah)—name of girl in this folktale

cailin (caw´ leen)—girl

Other words in the story:

hedgerow—a long, continuous hedge

ye—you

ragweed—a weed with a bright yellow flower

fortnight—two weeks

garter—a soft elastic band for holding up stockings

In a small farming village in Ireland lived a young girl with long red braids and a head full of wishes and dreams. Everyone called her Breda. That was short for Bridget.

One fair afternoon, when all her chores were done, Breda headed toward an emerald field near her house. She waved good-bye to her mother who was peelin' potatoes. She waved good-bye to her dear father who was shearin' the sheep.

Gaily she skipped through the hedge opening at the edge of her family's farm. Not long after, she heard a sound that made her stand as still as a stone wall.

"Tap, tap, tappity tap," sang a tiny hammer.

Following the sound, Breda tiptoed over to the corner of a neighbor's hedgerow. She held her breath and peeked over. Just as she'd thought.

"Good day to ye, little man," Breda chirped to the leprechaun she'd found. "I've caught ye off guard, have I, wee shoemaker?"

shearin' the sheep

"So ye have, my red-haired cailin," the leprechaun agreed. He tried to hide his surprise and annoyance. He straightened his apron and his three-cornered hat and kept right on tapping at the slipper he was repairing.

Breda had many a dream of finding a pot of gold, for her family had no money to spare.

"It's not every day I find a leprechaun. I mustn't lose my chance now," she thought.

Keeping her eye fixed on the leprechaun, lest he disappear, she dashed around the hedge. She grabbed hold of the wee man by his green coattails, upsetting his tiny wooden stool. "Now I've got ye!" she said. She flipped him around so as to carry him over her shoulder. She merrily chanted to herself,

"Wee leprechaun so sly and old,
It's time to take me to your gold."

"The treasure you speak of is long gone, miss," said the gray-bearded little man. Ye have the wrong leprechaun. I spend all of my days on shoemakin'. Those fairies, they wear out their slippers with all their dancin' and carryin' on."

"Don't be annoyin' me, little man, or I'll not ever be lettin' ye go. I'll take ye home and see what the townsfolk think of ye," Breda said. She knew how tricky a leprechaun could be.

"Very well, very well," said the leprechaun, wiggling about until he lay in Breda's arms like a large baby. "I'll take ye to the gold. Point your bare toes in the direction of the field of ragweed up ahead."

In the distance Breda could see a field filled with the bright yellow caps of the ragweed.

Though her feet were mighty sore and her arms were aching, Breda kept a strong hold on the leprechaun. All the while she thought of gold coins and of her family eating a hearty meal three times a day.

ragweed caps

She happily chanted to herself,

"Wee leprechaun so sly and old,
It's time to take me to your gold."

"Right here it is!" shouted the leprechaun. "Right here under this ragweed plant is where it's buried. Go ahead now. Dig it up, if ye must."

"Dig it up?" said Breda, setting the leprechaun down. "Oh, heaven be blessed, I have no shovel. Am I meant to spend a fortnight digging with my hands in this hard soil?"

"Now ye know the hiding place, I expect it won't do ye no harm to fetch a shovel!" exclaimed the leprechaun, brushing off his coat and settling his hat on his head.

"I suppose you're right," said Breda. She smiled as an idea formed in her mind. "I'll mark the weed with my red garter. Then I'll know just the spot I'll need to be diggin'."

With that, she spun around and headed back to the farmhouse just as fast as she could run over the rock-strewn grass.

As she returned with the shovel, Breda's spirits were soaring. She sang right out loud as she marched along,

"Wee leprechaun so sly and old,
It's time for me to have your gold."

As soon as she set foot in the field of ragweed, the song died on her lips. Around every single ragweed plant—the whole lot of them—was a bright red garter, blowing gaily in the soft wind. As for the little leprechaun, he was nowhere in sight.

"He's tricked me!" Breda moaned.

Breda dug under a ragweed plant that seemed to be the one the leprechaun had pointed out to her, but there was no gold to be found. She frantically dug here and there for all the rest of the day. It grew so dark she could see her shovel no more. Still, she was no closer to the gold.

From that day on, whenever Breda finished her chores on the farm, she would wander about, peeking over hedgerows, checking under leaves, and peering into the doorways of old castles. Everywhere she went, she'd be listening for the ever-so-faint tapping of the leprechaun's tiny hammer.

Questions about Leprechauns

1. Leprechauns are said to be ________.

   ◯ clerks ◯ weavers

   ◯ shoemakers ◯ dairy farmers

2. What kind of treasure does each leprechaun have?

   ____

3. What sound led Breda to the leprechaun?

   ____

4. How did the leprechaun feel when Breda found him?

   ____

   ____

5. How did the leprechaun trick Breda?

   ____

   ____

6. What parts of this story could be true?

   ____

   ____

7. What parts of this story are make-believe? How do you know?

   ____

   ____

   ____

Tell It in Order

Draw a map of the story. Include each of the places where important events happened. Then draw Breda's path as she moves through the story.

What Does It Mean?

Fill in the circle next to the correct meaning for each bolded word.

1. In this story, the word ***emerald*** means
   Ⓐ yellow
   Ⓑ precious stone
   Ⓒ bright green

2. Another word for ***boundaries*** is
   Ⓐ edges
   Ⓑ books
   Ⓒ shamrocks

3. A ***slipper*** is something you
   Ⓐ drink
   Ⓑ wear
   Ⓒ sleep on

4. At a ***hearty*** meal there is
   Ⓐ nothing to eat
   Ⓑ little to eat
   Ⓒ plenty to eat

5. A ***faint*** sound is
   Ⓐ loud and easy to hear
   Ⓑ musical
   Ⓒ quiet and hard to hear

6. In this story, the word ***charm*** means
   Ⓐ an object with a magic power
   Ⓑ a good smell
   Ⓒ a map or poster

7. When you ***chant*** you
   Ⓐ do something that isn't fair
   Ⓑ repeat a simple poem or song over and over again
   Ⓒ win first place

8. Another word for ***wander*** is
   Ⓐ roam
   Ⓑ ramble
   Ⓒ cry

9. If you are ***sly*** you are
   Ⓐ gentle and sweet
   Ⓑ big and strong
   Ⓒ clever and cunning

10. In this story, the word ***ragweed*** means
    Ⓐ old clothes
    Ⓑ a kind of plant
    Ⓒ a thick stew

Long Vowel Sounds

A. Circle the words that contain the **long i** sound.

weight	height	aisle
white	split	list
signal	might	willow
reply	happy	style

B. Circle the words that contain the **long o** sound.

stopped	home	groan
ghost	smooth	lovely
rough	stone	rainbow
gold	most	moss

C. Find long vowel words in the story that answer each clue.

1. Leprechauns are found in stories told by ________________ people.
2. Leprechauns wear ____________-colored clothing.
3. Legend says that leprechauns have hidden treasures of ______________.
4. This vegetable was very important in Ireland. ____________________
5. A wall or a house could be made of ____________________.
6. A leprechaun is a tiny creature. Another word for *tiny* is ______________.
7. A story that appears in one's sleep is called a ____________________.
8. Leprechauns are said to be tricky. Another word for *tricky* is ___________.

Similes

At one point in the story, Breda stands "as still as a stone wall." This is called a **simile**. A simile is a comparison between two items using the word *like* or *as.* Complete these similes using your own ideas.

1. as tricky as ______________________________
2. as small as ______________________________
3. as cold as ______________________________
4. as gentle as ______________________________
5. as smart as ______________________________
6. run like ______________________________
7. cry like ______________________________
8. sing like ______________________________
9. grow like ______________________________
10. sleep like ______________________________

Word Scramble

Unscramble the words below from the story. Then unscramble the letters in the circles to find one of the leprechaun's magic gifts.

lohsev ___ ___ ___ ___ ___ (___)

gedlne ___ ___ (___) ___ ___ ___

march (___) ___ ___ ___ ___

deegh ___ ___ (___) ___ ___

lelwoy ___ ___ ___ ___ (___) ___

sturaree ___ ___ ___ ___ ___ (___) ___ ___

cublek ___ ___ ___ (___) ___ ___

osshe ___ ___ (___) ___ ___

___ ___ ___ ___   ___ ___ ___ ___

Grandma Moses

A tiny old lady sits at a small table. Her white hair is neatly pinned in a bun on the top of her head. She holds a paintbrush in her hand. A piece of pressed board lies flat on the table in front of her. Her wrinkled face wears a dreamy expression. At the moment she is not working. Her face is turned toward the window, but her eyes are closed. She is looking far into the past. The warm June breeze of a New York summer touches her cheek, but she does not feel it. She is watching snowflakes swirl around her farmhouse in the hills of Virginia. She is remembering the past.

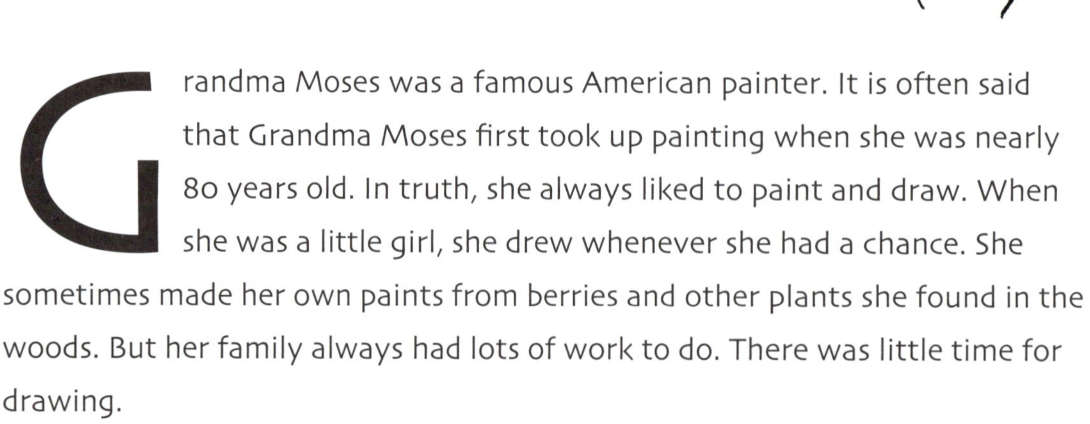

Grandma Moses was a famous American painter. It is often said that Grandma Moses first took up painting when she was nearly 80 years old. In truth, she always liked to paint and draw. When she was a little girl, she drew whenever she had a chance. She sometimes made her own paints from berries and other plants she found in the woods. But her family always had lots of work to do. There was little time for drawing.

When Grandma Moses was young, she wasn't called Grandma, of course. Her name was Anna Mary Robertson. She lived with her family on a farm in upstate New York. Anna Mary was a happy child who liked school and chores. She learned to do all kinds of housework. She sewed and baked. She helped her father collect sap from the maple trees and make it into syrup. She raised chickens, and she learned to churn delicious butter.

When Anna Mary was 27 years old, she married Thomas Moses. She and Thomas moved to Virginia. Here they raised dairy cows. Anna Mary made pounds and pounds of her famous butter. She sold the butter for fifty cents a pound. This was much more than butter usually cost. It must have been awfully good butter! Over the years Thomas and Anna Mary had five children. Anna Mary was a doting mother. She played with her children, but she also taught them to work. They had a happy life.

After 18 years in Virginia, Thomas and Anna Mary moved back to New York. Thomas worked the farm they bought. Anna Mary looked after her family. She still liked to paint and draw. She sometimes painted pretty scenes on household objects. Her family enjoyed her pictures, but she did not think they were very good.

As the years went by, the children grew up and moved away from home. Anna Mary and Thomas were lonely. They asked their youngest son, Hugh, and his new wife, Dorothy, to come live with them. This was a good thing, because in 1927 Thomas died of a heart attack.

Anna Mary missed her husband. She was glad that she had children and grandchildren to enjoy. They kept her busy and happy. For a time she entertained herself by stitching needlework pictures. But as she grew older her fingers were stiff. It was hard to hold the needle. She decided to try painting again to see if that would be easier.

Soon Anna Mary realized that painting brought her great joy. She would close her eyes or gaze off into space and recall a happy time from her life. She would remember helping her father collect maple sap. She would think of Christmastime when her own children were young.

She would try to create every detail of the scene in her mind. She would see the people, the farm buildings, and the animals. She would picture the blue mountains and the softly falling snow. When she had fixed the scene firmly in her mind, she began to paint.

Anna Mary painted many of these homey country scenes. Her friends and family members loved the paintings. Anna Mary gave them away as gifts. Hugh hung several of the paintings in the local drugstore.

One day a stranger came into the store. He bought every one of Anna Mary's paintings. He asked where she lived. He wanted to meet her. He thought her paintings were special. He visited with her and bought 10 more paintings. He took her paintings to New York City and showed them to some art dealers. One of these dealers, Dr. Kallir, liked the paintings. He hung some of them in his gallery. The newspaper did a story about the art show. The reporter called Anna Mary "Grandma Moses." From then on almost everyone used that nickname.

Grandma Moses kept on painting. Her paintings got better, and they got more popular. Everyone liked the scenes of a simple country life. The pictures were cheerful, warm, and full of life, just like Grandma herself.

Soon Grandma Moses was downright famous. She sold her paintings for lots of money. She was interviewed on television. She was even invited to the White House to meet President Truman!

Grandma Moses lived to be 101 years old. She left behind a joyful collection of pictures that still touch the heart. They are pictures that tell about country life in America more than 100 years ago. They are the pictures Anna Mary saw when she closed her eyes and remembered.

Skills: Recalling Details; Making Inferences

Questions about Grandma Moses

1. Why didn't Anna Mary have a lot of time to draw when she was a little girl?

____

____

2. When Anna Mary was a young woman, she sold ________.

- ◯ buttons
- ◯ butter
- ◯ cookies
- ◯ candies

3. How did Anna Mary get the nickname "Grandma Moses"?

____

____

4. What can we learn from looking at Grandma's paintings?

____

____

5. How do you think Grandma Moses felt about her life?

____

____

____

6. Make an **X** by each item that the story does not tell about.

_____ Anna Mary's brothers and sisters
_____ the kinds of pictures Grandma painted
_____ how to make butter
_____ Grandma's favorite kind of music
_____ how Grandma's paintings became famous

Reading with Expression

Here is the introduction to the biography of Grandma Moses. The author wrote it in a different tone from the rest of the article. The author wanted you to get a feeling about Grandma Moses before you began to read the biography.

Read the introduction aloud. Practice reading with feeling. Then read the introduction to someone else.

A tiny old lady sits at a small table. Her white hair is neatly pinned in a bun on the top of her head. She holds a paintbrush in her hand. A piece of pressed board lies flat on the table in front of her. Her wrinkled face wears a dreamy expression. At the moment, she is not working. Her face is turned toward the window, but her eyes are closed. She is looking far into the past. The warm June breeze of a New York summer touches her cheek, but she does not feel it. She is watching snowflakes swirl around her farmhouse in the hills of Virginia. She is remembering the past.

What Does It Mean?

Write each word on the line after its meaning.

scene	gallery
downright	needlework
dealer	homey
churn	dairy
interview	details

1. to stir and shake cream in order to make butter ______________________
2. comfortable and friendly ______________________
3. completely ______________________
4. small parts ______________________
5. a place where paintings are shown to the public ______________________
6. a meeting for the purpose of sharing information ______________________
7. a person who buys and sells things ______________________
8. a view of people or places ______________________
9. having to do with milk production ______________________
10. sewing or embroidery ______________________

Pronouns

A **pronoun** is a word that takes the place of a noun.
Rewrite each sentence using a pronoun in place of each underlined word or phrase.

her	he	it
they	us	him
we	them	she

1. Grandma made butter every day.

____

2. Grandma's pictures tell stories about Grandma's life.

____

3. Grandma enjoyed the children.

____

4. Sarah and I like to paint pictures too.

____

5. Sarah gave a picture to Wally and Mike.

____

6. Wally and Mike liked the picture very much.

____

7. Mike asked Sarah for a ride to school.

____

8. Joe got a ride with Wally.

____

A Timeline

Read the events in Grandma Moses's life. Write the letters in the correct order on the timeline. Draw something to represent each event.

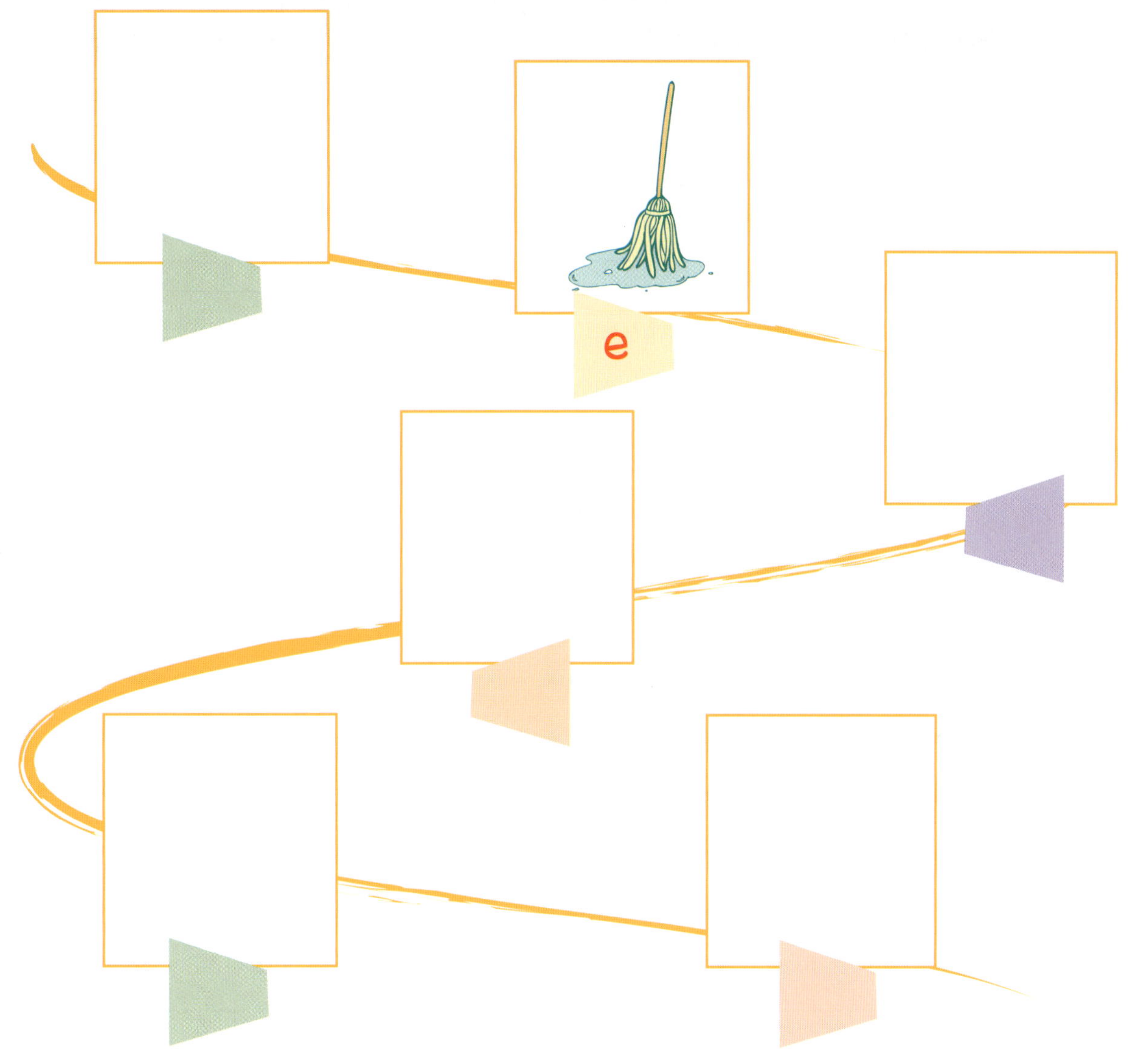

a After Thomas died, Anna Mary made pictures with needlework.

b As an old woman, Anna Mary became famous for her paintings.

c When she was 27, Anna Mary married Thomas Moses.

d As a young girl, Anna Mary made her own paints from berries and plants.

e Anna Mary learned to do all kinds of housework.

f Anna Mary was a loving mother to her five children.

Categories

Fill in each category of the chart using words that begin with the letters given.

	colors	animals	plants	foods
r				
p				
b				
g				

Understanding What You Read

Fill in the circle next to the correct answer.

1. Grandma Moses mostly painted pictures of _______.

   Ⓐ famous people
   Ⓑ scenes she remembered from her life
   Ⓒ skyscrapers
   Ⓓ the ocean

2. Anna Mary turned from needlework to painting because _______.

   Ⓐ she thought it might be easier for her stiff fingers
   Ⓑ she thought paintings were prettier
   Ⓒ she ran out of thread for her needlework
   Ⓓ her children gave her a set of paints

3. Grandma Moses was invited to meet _______.

   Ⓐ President Lincoln
   Ⓑ President Truman
   Ⓒ President Kennedy
   Ⓓ President Bush

4. As a young girl, Anna Mary helped her father _______.

   Ⓐ raise vegetables
   Ⓑ pick fruit
   Ⓒ make maple syrup
   Ⓓ cut firewood

5. Anna Mary's son took some of her paintings to display in a nearby _______.

   Ⓐ grocery store
   Ⓑ clothing store
   Ⓒ shoe store
   Ⓓ drugstore

6. Grandma Moses lived to be _______.

   Ⓐ 65 years old
   Ⓑ 80 years old
   Ⓒ 90 years old
   Ⓓ 101 years old

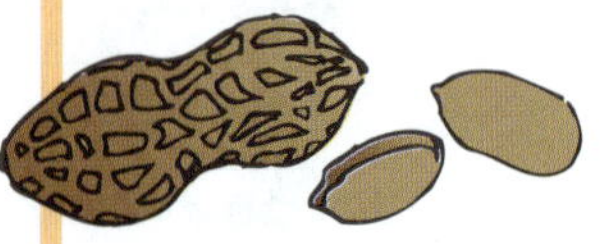

Nuts About Peanuts

"Peanuts! Get your red-hot peanuts."

Americans have loved the crunchy taste of peanuts ever since 1870. That was the year P. T. Barnum introduced hot peanuts as a snack. He sold them at his circus. Soon everyone wanted peanuts to eat!

But many people around the world ate peanuts long before that. Peanuts have been a popular food in Africa for hundreds of years. In South America, scientists found clay pots shaped like peanuts. These pots were over 3,000 years old! Some of the pots were filled with dried peanuts. Ancient dried peanuts have also been found in China.

Enslaved Africans probably brought peanuts to this country in the 1700s. Peanuts grew very well in the southern United States. The sandy soil and moist climate was good for peanuts. At first farmers grew peanuts as food for their livestock.

But one man thought that peanuts could be useful in other ways. His name was George Washington Carver. He was born near the end of the Civil War. His parents were enslaved. From boyhood, George had a great interest in nature. He especially liked plants. He worked hard and got an education. He became a botanist. A botanist is a scientist who studies plants.

George Washington Carver won many awards for his research. He studied peanuts, sweet potatoes, and many other plants.

Carver spent many years working with peanuts. He used peanuts to create more than three hundred products. These items include soap, ink, plastic, and paint. George Washington Carver is famous for this work. There is a national monument to him in Missouri where he was born. He helped to make peanuts an important crop.

Peanuts are not really nuts. They are legumes. Peas and beans are also legumes. Legumes are seeds that grow in pods. But peanuts have a special difference. The seedpods of the peanut develop beneath the ground.

The peanut plant is very bushy and green. It produces many small yellow blossoms. When the blossoms die, their stems bend down toward the ground. They begin to dig into the soil. A seedpod grows on the tip of each stem. When the peanuts are ripe, they are dug out of the ground. A special tractor is used for this job. The peanuts must be harvested at just the right time. If the soil is too wet or too dry, many of the peanuts will remain stuck in the ground. After harvesting, peanuts are dried. Then they are sent to factories. There they are packaged as snacks or made into other products.

Next time you go to a circus or a baseball game, listen carefully. You may hear someone shouting, "Peanuts! Get your red-hot peanuts!"

Fast Facts About Peanuts

Peanuts are good for you. They are a good source of protein. They contain vitamin E. Vitamin E may help prevent cancer. Peanuts are also a good source of some B vitamins.

Ecuador is a small country. It is in South America. People recently went there to study peanuts. They found more than two hundred different kinds of peanuts growing there. Ecuador has more kinds of peanut plants than any country in the world.

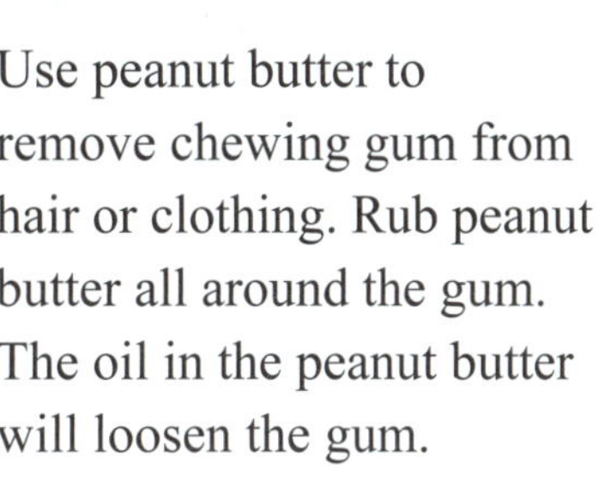

Use peanut butter to remove chewing gum from hair or clothing. Rub peanut butter all around the gum. The oil in the peanut butter will loosen the gum.

Peanuts are sometimes called "goobers." This nickname comes from the African word for peanut, *nguba.*

U.S. President Jimmy Carter was once a peanut farmer. When he was a young boy he lived on a farm. He helped his father raise peanuts. Jimmy sold boiled peanuts at a roadside stand. This was his only way to earn spending money.

Some people are allergic to peanuts! This is a very serious problem. People with this allergy must be careful not to eat any peanuts. They can't eat peanut butter or any other peanut products. Some people can get sick from just the smell of peanuts.

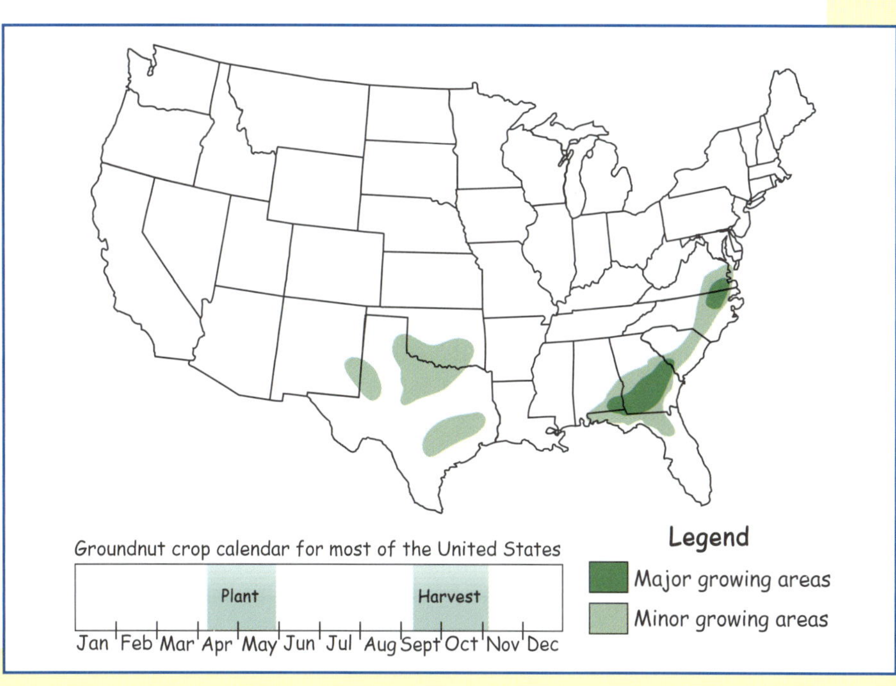

Peanut-growing areas of the United States

Peanut Butter

Many of the peanuts grown in the U.S. are used to make peanut butter. First, the peanuts are harvested and dried. Next, they are run across a screen to remove rocks and stems. After cleaning, the peanuts are shelled and roasted. Then they are cooled. Then they are rubbed gently between rubber belts to remove their skins. Finally, they are ground to a paste. Sugar, salt, and oil are sometimes added.

Peanut butter was invented around 1890. A doctor created it. He made it for his patients who had no teeth. He thought it would be a good food for these patients. It would give them protein. In 1904 peanut butter was sold at the World's Fair in St. Louis. It was a big hit. In 1922 peanut butter was packed in jars for the first time. This meant it could be sold in stores around the country.

Make Your Own Peanut Butter

- 1 cup of roasted, unsalted peanuts
- 1 to 3 tablespoons of peanut or vegetable oil
- salt

Grind peanuts in a bowl or food processor until finely chopped. Add oil one tablespoon at a time. Blend until smooth. Add salt to your taste. Store in a tightly covered container in the refrigerator. It will stay fresh for about two weeks.

Questions about Nuts About Peanuts

1. Where and when were peanuts first sold in the United States?
   - ◯ at a fair in 1900
   - ◯ at a circus in 1870
   - ◯ at a movie theater in 1950
   - ◯ at a baseball game in 1820

2. What country is home to the most different kinds of peanut plants?

   ____

3. Name three states where peanuts are grown.

   __________ __________ __________

4. What is a legume?

   ____

   ____

5. How are peanuts different from other legumes?

   ____

   ____

6. Why can't peanuts be harvested when the ground is very wet or very dry?

   ____

   ____

7. Who is famous for his research with peanuts?

   ____

8. Name at least three products that can be made with peanuts.

   __________ __________ __________

Tell It in Order

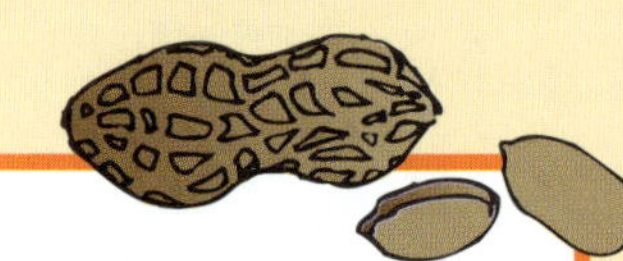

Write the steps for making peanut butter in order. Leave out any steps that do not belong.

Then they are dried.

The skins are then removed.

Finally, they are ground into a paste.

Jimmy Carter sold peanuts as a boy.

After that, they are cleaned to remove rocks and stems.

The peanuts must first be harvested.

Next, they are shelled and roasted.

Some people are allergic to peanuts.

What Does It Mean?

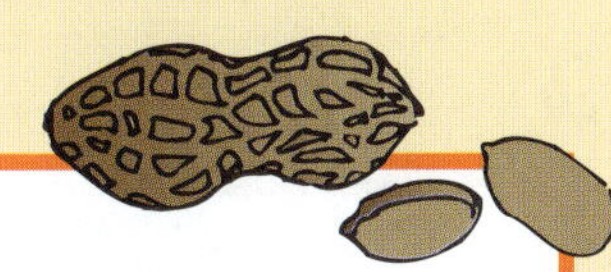

Complete the sentences using words from the word box.

Word Box

protein	roast	allergic
goober	legumes	vitamins
climate	harvest	factory
botanist	Ecuador	

1. ________________ is a nickname for the peanut.
2. ________________ are plants whose seeds grow in pods.
3. ________________ is a country in South America.
4. ________________ and ________________ are nutrients found in foods.
5. A ____________________ is a scientist who studies plants.
6. A ____________________ is a place where products are made.
7. Peanuts make Pamela sick because she is ________________ to them.
8. The ____________________ in the desert is hot and dry.
9. ____________________ means to gather crops from the field.
10. Dad put the potatoes in the oven to ____________________.

Fantastic Fact

The amount of peanut butter eaten each year in the United States (500 million pounds) is enough to cover the floor of the Grand Canyon.

Adverbs Tell How

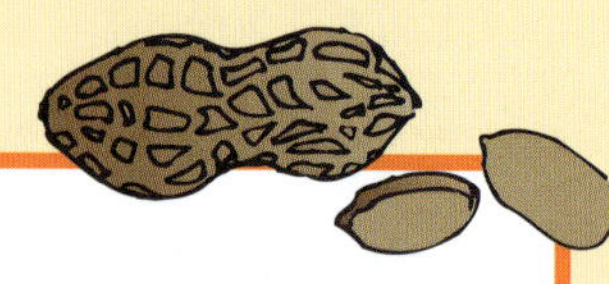

An **adverb** is a word that tells how an action was done.

Use one phrase from each column to create a sentence that makes sense. Write the sentence on the lines below. Then circle the adverb in each sentence.

The dog howled	gently	at the recital.
The pizza baked	loudly	in the hot oven.
Tony sang	carefully	around the baby.
Esther sat	beautifully	on the antique chair.
Arthur wrapped the blanket	quickly	at the moon.

1. ______________________________

2. ______________________________

3. ______________________________

4. ______________________________

5. ______________________________

Reference Skills

Use a dictionary, an encyclopedia, or an almanac to find the correct answers.

1. Africa is a ________.
   - ◯ country
   - ◯ continent
   - ◯ city

2. The Civil War in the United States began in the year ________.
   - ◯ 1776
   - ◯ 1941
   - ◯ 1861

3. What is the capital of Missouri?

4. President Jimmy Carter was born in the state of ________________________ .

5. Find one fact about China. ____

   ____

6. What is a blossom? ____

   ____

Fantastic Fact

The average American child will eat 1,500 peanut butter sandwiches by the time she or he graduates from high school.

Fact or Opinion?

A **fact** tells information that is true. An **opinion** tells about someone's thoughts or feelings.

A. Decide whether each sentence states a fact or gives an opinion.

1. Peanuts are delicious. — fact opinion
2. Peanut butter is made from peanuts. — fact opinion
3. George Washington Carver was a scientist. — fact opinion
4. Ecuador is the best place to go for a vacation. — fact opinion
5. It is fun to go to the circus. — fact opinion
6. Peanuts are legumes. — fact opinion
7. Some people are allergic to peanuts. — fact opinion
8. St. Louis is in Missouri. — fact opinion
9. Peanut butter tastes good with jelly. — fact opinion
10. Boiled peanuts taste better than roasted peanuts. — fact opinion

B. Write one fact and one opinion of your own. Ask a family member to tell which is which.

1. ______________________________

____

____

2. ______________________________

____

____

The Legend of
Blackbeard the Pirate

Blackbeard the pirate was the fiercest pirate who ever lived. He had a sailing ship armed with forty cannons. He roamed the southern coast of what is now the United States. During a two-year period from 1716 to 1718, he spread a path of fear and destruction. He flew a flag with a skull and crossbones. He captured ships. He stole and plundered at will. The people were very frightened of him.

Blackbeard was a real man. His real name was Edward. Edward, however, is not a scary enough name for a pirate. So he allowed his dark beard to grow long and bushy. This gave him a more frightening appearance and a more suitable nickname.

Blackbeard did other things to make himself look evil. He braided his beard and tied it full of red ribbons. He wore six pistols slung across his chest. He wore a black hat on his head. Still, he was not satisfied. He thought he did not look dreadful enough. He wanted to strike terror in the hearts of his victims. So he took some fuses from his cannons. These were pieces of string that had been soaked in a mixture of water and gunpowder. He stuck the ends of these fuses under his hat so they stuck out around his face. Then he lit the fuses with a candle. The fuses sputtered and smoked. They gave off a ghostly light and a terrible gassy smell. Now Blackbeard was content. Surely anyone he attacked would faint at the very sight of him. He would not even have to fight.

And, indeed, this often happened. When Blackbeard's ship came into view, other ships often surrendered. The captains and crews were willing to give Blackbeard their cargoes of sugar, silver, spices, and gold in exchange for their lives. Sometimes he killed some of his captives. He released the others, knowing they would tell stories of his cruelty. If a captive was wearing a ring that he wanted, Blackbeard would simply chop off the finger to get the ring. News of these gruesome acts spread quickly. This was part of Blackbeard's plan. He wanted everyone to tremble at the very sound of his name.

This fear gave Blackbeard great power. Once he held a whole city captive. He sailed into the harbor at Charleston, South Carolina. He captured several ships. He took many prisoners. He said he would pound the city with his cannons unless he got what he wanted. He claimed that he would murder his captives and burn the ships. Then he would burn the city too. Everyone was in a panic. The citizens fled into the countryside. They knew that Blackbeard was mean and evil enough to carry out these threats.

The governor of South Carolina was ready to give Blackbeard whatever he wanted. He offered money and jewels. But Blackbeard wanted something else. He wanted medicines. Some of his crewmen were sick. They could not get medicines at sea. The governor sent a large trunk of medicines to Blackbeard's ship. Once the trunk was on board, Blackbeard calmly sailed away.

The citizens began to get very angry. They wanted someone to capture Blackbeard. The governor of Virginia understood the problem. Cargo could not go in and out of the harbors because all of the ships' captains were afraid.

The governor decided to take action. He knew there were warships nearby. These ships were strong enough to attack Blackbeard. But the warships were slow and heavy. He needed ships that could make a surprise attack. This meant ships that could sail fast. The governor didn't want anyone to know his plans. He was afraid that someone would tell Blackbeard. He secretly used his own money to buy two light ships called "sloops." He hired two crews of sailors from the warships. He made the sailors promise not to tell anyone about the plan. He placed Lieutenant Robert Maynard in command of the mission. The two sloops set off on November 17, 1718. They were determined to catch Blackbeard.

They found Blackbeard hiding in his usual spot, an inlet along Ocracoke Island. This inlet was like a stream that ran between the island and a sandbar. A sloop entered from each end of the inlet. Blackbeard tried to escape, but his ship ran aground.

This was the moment Maynard and his men had been waiting for. They swarmed onto Blackbeard's ship, shooting and swinging their swords. A wild fight took place. Blackbeard and his men fought for their lives. Smoke from cannon and pistol fire swirled around the deck. The noise was deafening. At last, Maynard's men overpowered the pirate crew. Blackbeard himself fell dead on the ship's deck. He had more than twenty-five wounds in his body. Five of them were from pistol shots!

Blackbeard's reign of terror had come to an end.

Skills: Recalling Details; Making Inferences; Drawing on Personal Experiences

Questions about

The Legend of
Blackbeard the Pirate

1. Why did Blackbeard want to look scary?

2. What did Blackbeard do to make himself look scary?

   - ◯ He wore a hat made of bearskin.
   - ◯ He wore a necklace made of bones.
   - ◯ He put lit fuses in his beard.
   - ◯ He painted a spider on his face.

3. What did Blackbeard demand from the people of Charleston? Why?

4. Why didn't the governor send the warships after Blackbeard?

5. List three words that describe Blackbeard.

6. When Blackbeard attacked Charleston, the people were very frightened. Think of a time when you felt afraid. Write about the experience.

Tell It in Order

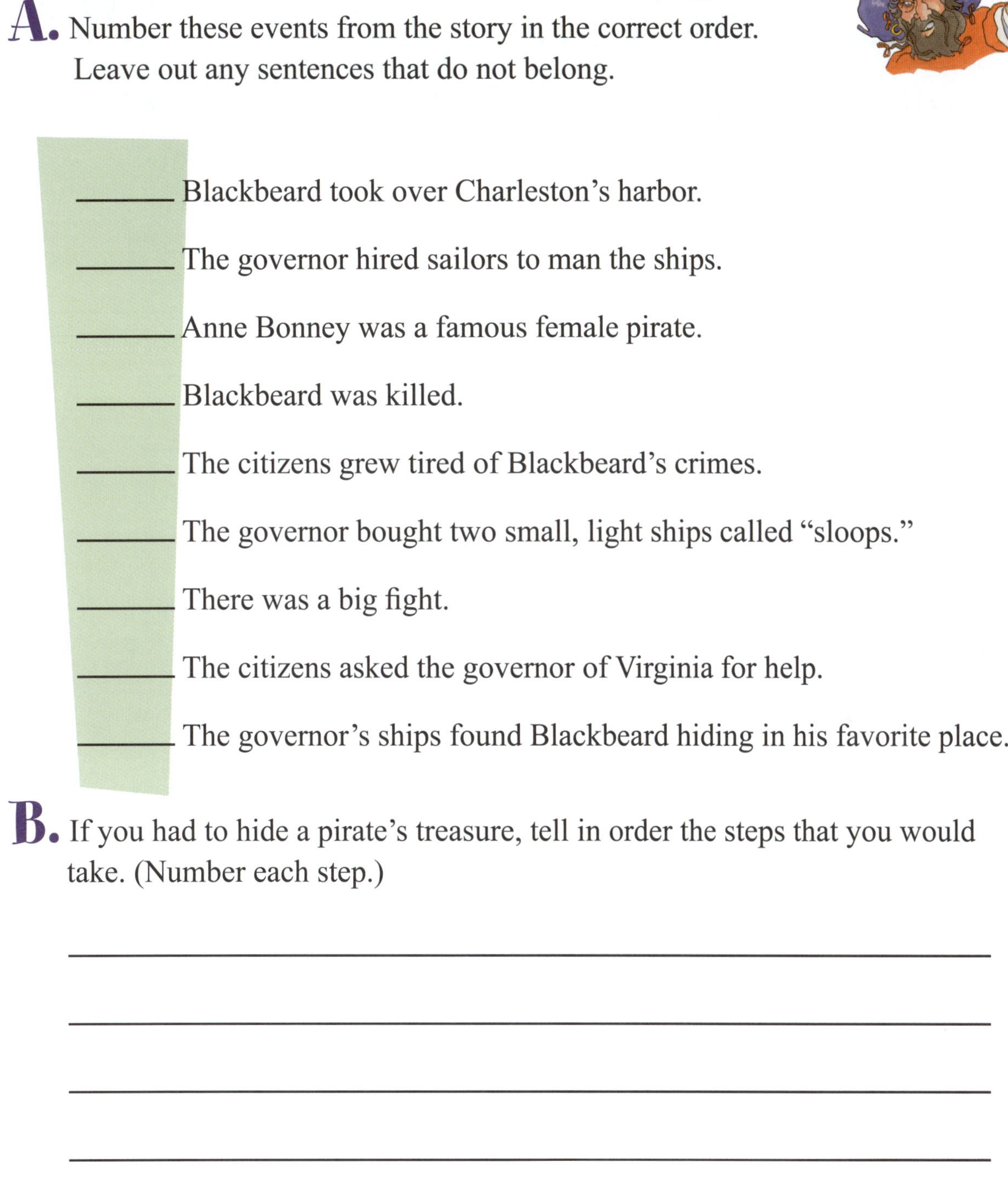

A. Number these events from the story in the correct order. Leave out any sentences that do not belong.

_______ Blackbeard took over Charleston's harbor.

_______ The governor hired sailors to man the ships.

_______ Anne Bonney was a famous female pirate.

_______ Blackbeard was killed.

_______ The citizens grew tired of Blackbeard's crimes.

_______ The governor bought two small, light ships called "sloops."

_______ There was a big fight.

_______ The citizens asked the governor of Virginia for help.

_______ The governor's ships found Blackbeard hiding in his favorite place.

B. If you had to hide a pirate's treasure, tell in order the steps that you would take. (Number each step.)

____

____

____

____

____

____

____

What Does It Mean?

1. Cross out the word that does not belong in each group.

evil	stole	cargo	gruesome
mean	robbed	merchandise	pleasant
kind	plundered	sailors	frightful
wicked	gave	freight	gory

2. The word *captive* in this story means ______.

Ⓐ princess
Ⓑ prisoner
Ⓒ principal

3. Fill in the circle beside each item you would probably find in a harbor.

Ⓐ a boat
Ⓑ an airliner
Ⓒ a dock
Ⓓ an anchor

4. A *fuse* is a string or wick that is soaked with explosive material.
It is used to ______.

Ⓐ hoist a sail
Ⓑ tie a shoe
Ⓒ light a cannon

5. Many pirate ships flew a flag that looked like this:  .
It was called ______.

Ⓐ the skull and crossbones
Ⓑ the head and arm bones
Ⓒ the skeleton

Alphabetical Order

A. Write these words from the story in alphabetical order.

cannon ____________________

ship ____________________

flag ____________________

beard ____________________

ribbons ____________________

gunpowder ____________________

candle ____________________

sugar ____________________

gold ____________________

treasure ____________________

hat ____________________

silver ____________________

B. Write a paragraph telling what you think happened to Blackbeard's treasure.

____

____

____

____

____

____

____

Homophones

Homophones are words that sound alike but have different meanings and different spellings.

A. Write a homophone for each word below.

1. sale	____________	6. pane	____________
2. blew	____________	7. waist	____________
3. sent	____________	8. steal	____________
4. beech	____________	9. knot	____________
5. prey	____________	10. weak	____________

B. Write two sentences. Use a homophone pair in each sentence. For example:

I ***pray*** that the deer will not ***prey*** on my vegetable garden this year.

1. ____

____

____

2. ____

____

____

Fantastic Fact

Pirates had rules! Crew members signed documents and swore to uphold a code of honor.

Following Directions

Write the number of each box in front of the directions it illustrates.

_____ Circle the things that float. Make an **X** on the things that are alive.

_____ Draw a line under the things that you eat. Make an **X** on the things that can fly.

_____ Circle the things that you wear. Draw a line under each vehicle.

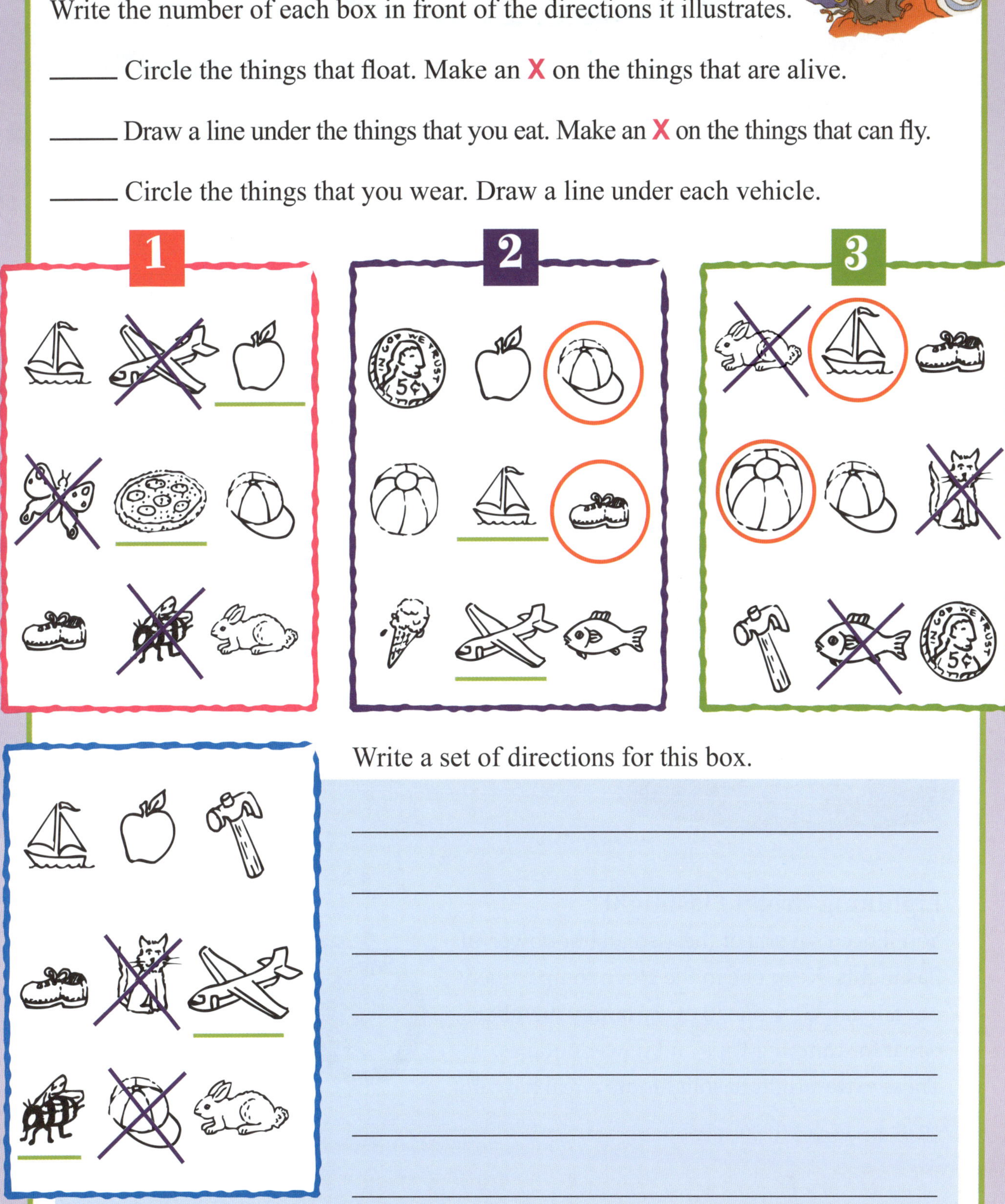

Write a set of directions for this box.

Shop at

Home

Paddle Popper

Use this specially designed popcorn pot to make loads of fresh, crunchy popcorn. It has a crank in the handle that turns a paddle inside the pot. The paddle keeps the kernels moving and prevents burning. The Paddle Popper makes a great gift!

Only $19.95

Teddy Bear Telephone

This cute telephone would be a fun addition for any room in your house. It is made of easy-to-clean plastic and is a full 16 inches tall. The phone features a touch-tone key pad and automatic redial. This popular item is selling fast, so order now!

$29.95

Lightning Bright Flashlight

You'll need several of these small but powerful flashlights. Keep one in the glove compartment of your car. Give one to every family member. Great for camping trips and power outages. These extra-bright flashlights are a real bargain!

$5.95 or 2 for $10.00

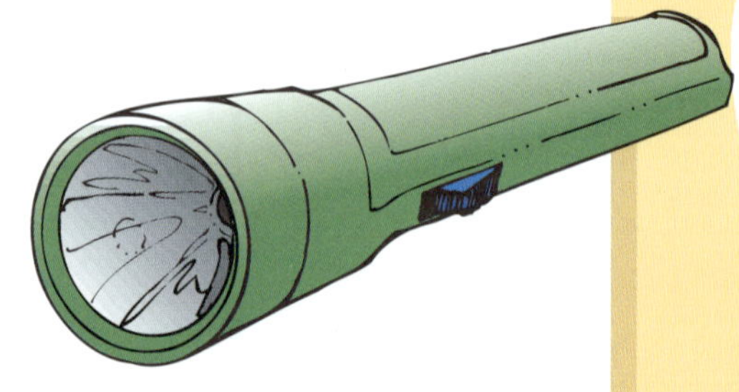

Questions about

Shop at Home

1. What three items are shown on the page of the Shop at Home catalog?

2. Which item would make the best gift for your parents? Why?

3. Which item would you most like to have? Why?

4. What words and phrases are used to make the reader want to buy each item?

   Paddle Popper

   Teddy Bear Telephone

   Lightning Bright Flashlight

5. Why do you think some people like to shop using catalogs?

Words That Sell

The Shop at Home catalog has a new product to sell. It is called a ***Snickadoodler***. Draw a picture and write a description of the Snickadoodler. Try to use words that will make everyone want to buy one!

The Story of
Shep

Long ago, on a cold winter night, a poor sheepherder came to the door of the small hospital in Fort Benton, Montana. A ragged-looking dog was at his heels. The sheepherder was very ill. The nurses at the hospital rushed him inside. They hurried him into bed. The doctor examined the sheepherder. He gave him some medicine. A kindly nurse found some food for the dog in the hospital kitchen.

The people at the hospital did all they could. But the sheepherder died from his illness. The nurses called his family. They asked that the sheepherder's body be sent to them by train. The sheepherder's loyal dog watched as his master's body was loaded onto the train. He whined as the door to the boxcar slid shut with a bang. As the train pulled out of the station, the old dog lay down near the tracks. He watched the train roll away into the distance.

When station employees tried to pet the dog, he growled and scrambled away. Because he was not very friendly, they tried to chase him away. He would move off, but never too far. Soon he was right back at the station's platform. He dug a hole beneath the platform for shelter from the cold.

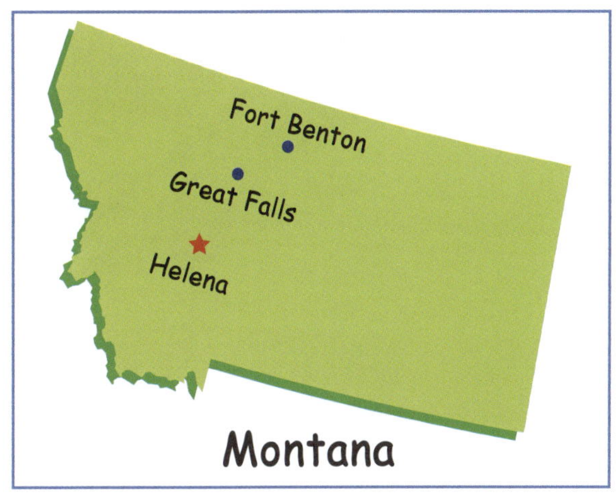

Trains came to Fort Benton four times every day. The dog was there to meet each one. He anxiously watched each passenger get off the train. Then, disappointed, he would return to his hole under the platform.

The stationmaster, a man named Ed, felt sorry for the dog. He named the dog Shep. Ed began to leave scraps of food and bowls of milk out for Shep. He encouraged the dog to come inside the station where it was warm. Finally this kindness overcame Shep's fear. Shep learned to trust Ed and the other railroad workers. He would come inside to get warm. But when the tracks hummed and the train whistle blew, Shep was back at his post.

For almost five years Shep kept his watch. He met every train. In the heat of summer, the bitter cold of winter, the slashing rains of spring, Shep was faithful. Four times every day, Shep was there to meet the trains.

Passengers who came to Fort Benton were interested in the dog. They wondered why he was always there, watching the trains come and go. Finally Ed decided to tell Shep's story. He wrote a little pamphlet that was sold to passengers for a small price. Newspapers shared Shep's inspiring story across the nation. Shep even appeared in the famous newspaper cartoon called "Ripley's Believe It or Not."

Many people wanted to adopt Shep, but he would not leave the train station. Day after day, he continued to wait and watch. Shep was very old when he died in 1942.

The people of Fort Benton were very sad. They wanted to do something special for Shep. Ed built a casket for Shep. The town held a funeral. The mayor and hundreds of townsfolk attended. The Boy Scout troop carried the casket to a hill overlooking the train station. The town of Fort Benton said a loving good-bye to the faithful dog.

But that is not the end of the story. You see, people were impressed by Shep's great loyalty. The pamphlet about Shep continued to sell. Ed decided to give the money from the sales to the Montana School for the Deaf and Blind. The money was called "The Shep Fund." The fund was used to pay for outings for the children at the school.

As the years went by, the people of Fort Benton kept the memory of Shep close to their hearts. On the fiftieth anniversary of his death, they decided to put up a monument to honor Shep. They raised money and had a beautiful bronze statue made. It is a statue of Shep. He stands looking toward the old train station, keeping his watch.

Today, visitors stroll through the park along the banks of the Missouri River. They stop to view the statue of Shep. They buy the pamphlet that tells the story of Shep's steadfast love for his master. They learn that The Shep Fund has grown to over two million dollars. It now helps to pay for programs and equipment at the Montana School for the Deaf and Blind.

Shep will never be forgotten. His story will be told again and again. The donations his story inspires will help many, many children for years to come.

Understanding What You Read

Fill in the circle next to the correct answer.

1. Shep's owner was a _____.
   - Ⓐ baker
   - Ⓑ firefighter
   - Ⓒ carpenter
   - Ⓓ sheepherder

2. Trains came to Fort Benton _____.
   - Ⓐ once a day
   - Ⓑ two times a day
   - Ⓒ four times a day
   - Ⓓ every two hours throughout the day

3. A statue honoring Shep stands on the banks of the _____.
   - Ⓐ Tennessee River
   - Ⓑ Hudson River
   - Ⓒ Potomac River
   - Ⓓ Missouri River

4. How did the people of Fort Benton feel when Shep died?
   - Ⓐ They were very happy.
   - Ⓑ They did not care.
   - Ⓒ They were sad.
   - Ⓓ They were angry.

5. Who fed Shep and earned his trust?
   - Ⓐ the train's engineer
   - Ⓑ the stationmaster
   - Ⓒ the school teacher
   - Ⓓ the mayor of Fort Benton

6. The Shep Fund has provided over _____ dollars for the Montana School for the Deaf and Blind.
   - Ⓐ ten thousand
   - Ⓑ one million
   - Ⓒ seven hundred
   - Ⓓ two million

Tell It in Order

Fill in each blank with ***before*** or ***after***.

1. The sheepherder went to the hospital ____________________ Shep died.

2. The people of Fort Benton felt sad ___________________ Shep died.

3. Shep stayed at the train station _____________________ his master died.

4. A nurse at the hospital fed Shep ____________________ he went to the train station.

5. Ed wrote a story about Shep _______________________ Shep died.

6. Fifty years _________________ Shep's death, the people built a monument for him.

7. Shep went inside the station to get warm _________________ Ed won his trust.

8. Many people wanted to adopt Shep __________________ he grew old.

Fantastic Fact

The United States and France have the most pet dogs—one dog for every three families. Germany and Switzerland have fewer pet dogs—only one dog for every ten families.

What Does It Mean?

A. Write each word on the line in front of its meaning.

scraps	sheepherder	anniversary	master	bronze
passenger	monument	donations	pamphlet	statue

1. ____________________ gifts of money
2. ____________________ a metal made by combining copper and tin
3. ____________________ bits of leftover food
4. ____________________ the form of a person or an animal carved in stone or cast in metal
5. ____________________ a person who rides on a bus, plane, or train
6. ____________________ the yearly occurrence of an event
7. ____________________ a person who watches over sheep as they graze
8. ____________________ a small booklet
9. ____________________ something set up in honor of the memory of a person, thing, or an event
10. ____________________ an owner

B. Choose a word from the list above to complete each sentence.

1. The generous ____________________ of the Parent Teacher Club made it possible for the fourth-graders to take a field trip to the state capital.
2. The ____________________ to George Washington towers over the mall in Washington, D.C.

Synonyms

A. Circle the two **synonyms** in each sentence.

1. The cold wind made Ralph feel chilly.
2. Maggie was afraid of the frightened dog.
3. The grimy little pig slept on a pile of dirty straw.
4. The sleepy little boy insisted that he wasn't tired.
5. The faithful dog was always loyal to his master.
6. The strong wind blew with a powerful force.
7. I like to wear tight jeans, but these are just a little too snug.
8. The weak old woman grew more feeble with each passing day.
9. Lydia pretended she was a bird and imagined herself flying above the treetops.
10. The huge football player ate a gigantic hamburger after practice.

B. Write two sentences of your own. Use a pair of synonyms in each sentence.

1. ____

____

2. ____

____

Sh-Sh-Sh...

A. Use the clues to find words that begin with ***sh***.

Hint: Some clues may have more than one answer.

1. a rickety cabin ______________________________
2. what a tree makes on a sunny day ______________________________
3. the opposite of *deep* ______________________________
4. what you wash your hair with ______________________________
5. a clover that is the emblem of Ireland ______________________________
6. to cut the hair of a sheep ______________________________
7. something that covers or protects ______________________________
8. a part of the body ______________________________
9. this covers a window ______________________________
10. some people prefer this to a bath ______________________________
11. something you wear ______________________________
12. what the earth does during an earthquake ______________________________
13. something you do when you're cold ______________________________

B. Think of two ***sh*** words of your own. Write clues to the words and then ask a family member or friend to guess the words.

1. ______________________________
2. ______________________________

Tracking Form

Topic	Color in each page you complete.					
The Lion and the Mouse	6	7	8	9	10	11
An Oregon Trail Diary	17	18	19	20	21	22
How to Make a Pair of Stilts	24	25				
The Old Woman Who Lived in a Vinegar Jug	29	30	31	32	33	34
Dick Whittington and His Wonderful Cat	42	43	44	45	46	47
Go Fly a Kite	51	52	53	54	55	56
Let's Go to the Movies	58	59				
The Three Sillies	65	66	67	68	69	70
Penguins, Pelicans, and Puffins	75	76	77	78	79	80
Blindfold Treasure Hunt	82	83				
Leprechauns	88	89	90	91	92	93
Grandma Moses	97	98	99	100	101	102
	103					
Nuts About Peanuts	107	108	109	110	111	112
The Legend of Blackbeard the Pirate	116	117	118	119	120	121
Shop at Home	123	124				
The Story of Shep	128	129	130	131	132	

Answer Key

Checking your child's work is an important part of learning. It allows you to see what your child knows well and what areas need more practice. It also provides an opportunity for you to help your child understand that making mistakes is a part of learning.

When an error is discovered, ask your child to look carefully at the question or problem. Errors often occur through misreading. Your child can quickly correct these errors. Help your child with items she or he finds difficult.

The answer key pages can be used in several ways:

- Remove the answer pages and give the book to your child. Go over the answers as each story and the accompanying activity pages are completed.
- Leave the answer pages in the book and give the practice pages to your child one story unit at a time.

Page 6

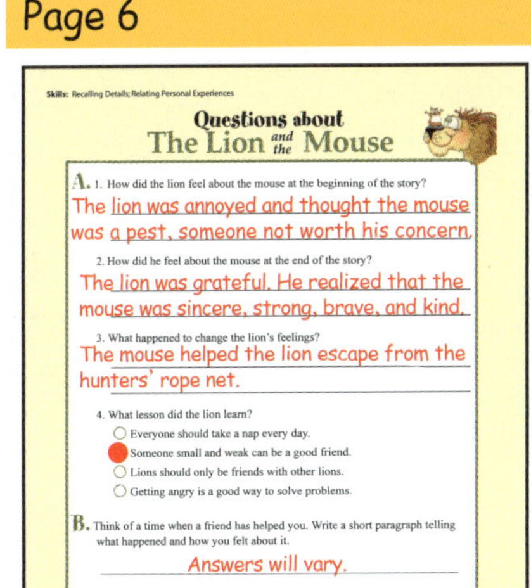

Skills: Recalling Details; Relating Personal Experiences

Questions about The Lion and the Mouse

A. 1. How did the lion feel about the mouse at the beginning of the story?
The lion was annoyed and thought the mouse was a pest, someone not worth his concern.

2. How did he feel about the mouse at the end of the story?
The lion was grateful. He realized that the mouse was sincere, strong, brave, and kind.

3. What happened to change the lion's feelings?
The mouse helped the lion escape from the hunters' rope net.

4. What lesson did the lion learn?
- Everyone should take a nap every day.
- ● Someone small and weak can be a good friend.
- Lions should only be friends with other lions.
- Getting angry is a good way to solve problems.

B. Think of a time when a friend has helped you. Write a short paragraph telling what happened and how you felt about it.
Answers will vary.

6 Reading • EMC 4532 • ©2005 by Evan-Moor Corp.

Page 7

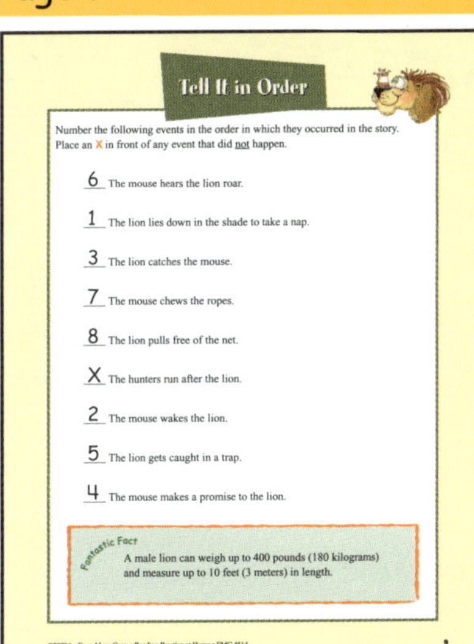

Tell It in Order

Number the following events in the order in which they occurred in the story. Place an X in front of any event that did not happen.

6 The mouse hears the lion roar.
1 The lion lies down in the shade to take a nap.
3 The lion catches the mouse.
7 The mouse chews the ropes.
8 The lion pulls free of the net.
X The hunters run after the lion.
2 The mouse wakes the lion.
5 The lion gets caught in a trap.
4 The mouse makes a promise to the lion.

Fantastic Fact: A male lion can weigh up to 400 pounds (180 kilograms) and measure up to 10 feet (3 meters) in length.

©2000 by Evan-Moor Corp. • Reading Practice at Home • EMC 4514 9

Page 8

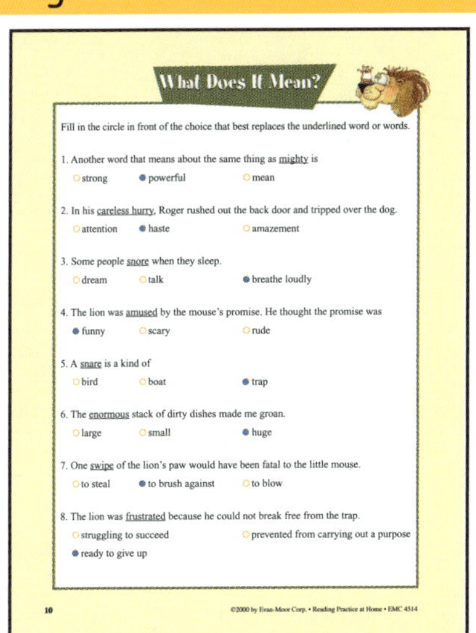

What Does It Mean?

Fill in the circle in front of the choice that best replaces the underlined word or words.

1. Another word that means about the same thing as mighty is
○ strong ● powerful ○ mean

2. In his careless hurry, Roger rushed out the back door and tripped over the dog.
○ attention ● haste ○ amazement

3. Some people snore when they sleep.
○ dream ○ talk ● breathe loudly

4. The lion was amused by the mouse's promise. He thought the promise was
● funny ○ scary ○ rude

5. A snare is a kind of
○ bird ○ boat ● trap

6. The enormous stack of dirty dishes made me groan.
○ large ○ small ● huge

7. One swipe of the lion's paw would have been fatal to the little mouse.
○ to steal ● to brush against ○ to blow

8. The lion was frustrated because he could not break free from the trap.
○ struggling to succeed ○ prevented from carrying out a purpose
● ready to give up

10 ©2000 by Evan-Moor Corp. • Reading Practice at Home • EMC 4514

Page 9

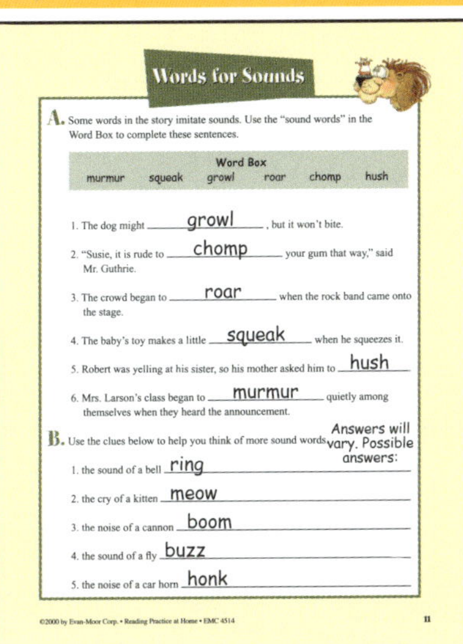

Words for Sounds

A. Some words in the story imitate sounds. Use the "sound words" in the Word Box to complete these sentences.

Word Box: murmur squeak growl roar chomp hush

1. The dog might growl, but it won't bite.
2. "Susie, it is rude to chomp your gum that way," said Mr. Guthrie.
3. The crowd began to roar when the rock band came onto the stage.
4. The baby's toy makes a little squeak when he squeezes it.
5. Robert was yelling at his sister, so his mother asked him to hush.
6. Mrs. Larson's class began to murmur quietly among themselves when they heard the announcement.

B. Use the clues below to help you think of more sound words. Answers will vary. Possible answers:

1. the sound of a bell ring
2. the cry of a kitten meow
3. the noise of a cannon boom
4. the sound of a fly buzz
5. the noise of a car horn honk

©2000 by Evan-Moor Corp. • Reading Practice at Home • EMC 4514 11

Page 10

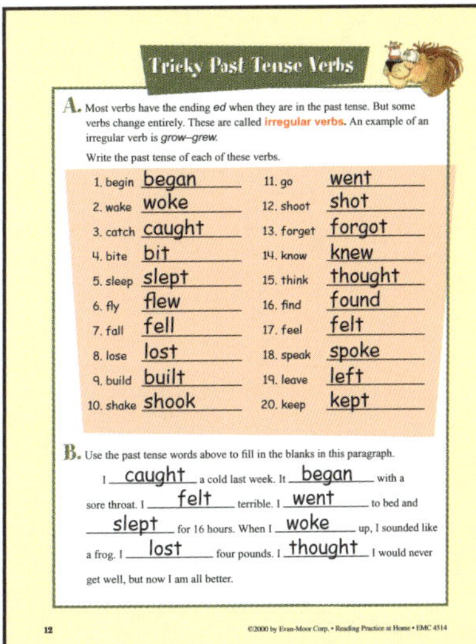

Tricky Past Tense Verbs

A. Most verbs have the ending *ed* when they are in the past tense. But some verbs change entirely. These are called irregular verbs. An example of an irregular verb is *grow–grew*.

Write the past tense of each of these verbs.

1. begin began	11. go went
2. wake woke	12. shoot shot
3. catch caught	13. forget forgot
4. bite bit	14. know knew
5. sleep slept	15. think thought
6. fly flew	16. find found
7. fall fell	17. feel felt
8. lose lost	18. speak spoke
9. build built	19. leave left
10. shake shook	20. keep kept

B. Use the past tense words above to fill in the blanks in this paragraph.

I caught a cold last week. It began with a sore throat. I felt terrible. I went to bed and slept for 16 hours. When I woke up, I sounded like a frog. I lost four pounds. I thought I would never get well, but now I am all better.

12 ©2000 by Evan-Moor Corp. • Reading Practice at Home • EMC 4514

Page 11

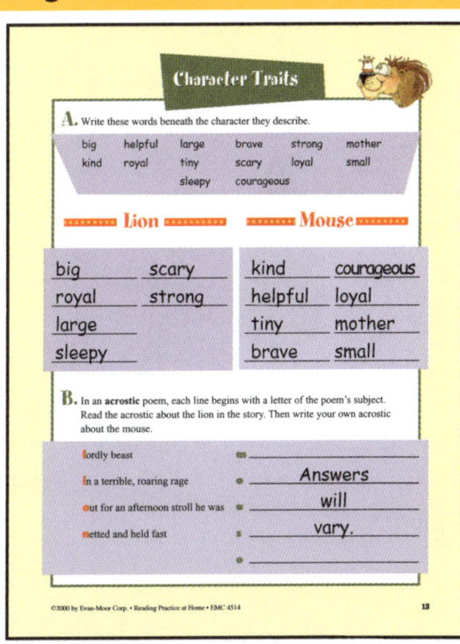

Character Traits

A. Write these words beneath the character they describe.

big helpful large brave strong mother kind royal tiny scary loyal small sleepy courageous

Lion		Mouse	
big	scary	kind	courageous
royal	strong	helpful	loyal
large		tiny	mother
sleepy		brave	small

B. In an acrostic poem, each line begins with a letter of the poem's subject. Read the acrostic about the lion in the story. Then write your own acrostic about the mouse.

lordly beast
in a terrible, roaring rage
out for an afternoon stroll he was
netted and held fast

Answers will vary.

©2000 by Evan-Moor Corp. • Reading Practice at Home • EMC 4514 13

Page 17

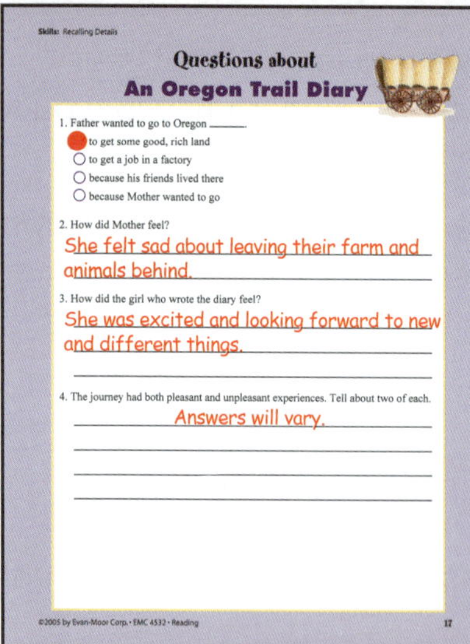

Skills: Recalling Details

Questions about An Oregon Trail Diary

1. Father wanted to go to Oregon ____.
   - ● to get some good, rich land
   - ○ to get a job in a factory
   - ○ because his friends lived there
   - ○ because Mother wanted to go
2. How did Mother feel?
   She felt sad about leaving their farm and animals behind.
3. How did the girl who wrote the diary feel?
   She was excited and looking forward to new and different things.
4. The journey had both pleasant and unpleasant experiences. Tell about two of each.
   Answers will vary.

©2005 by Evan-Moor Corp. • EMC 4532 • Reading 17

Page 18

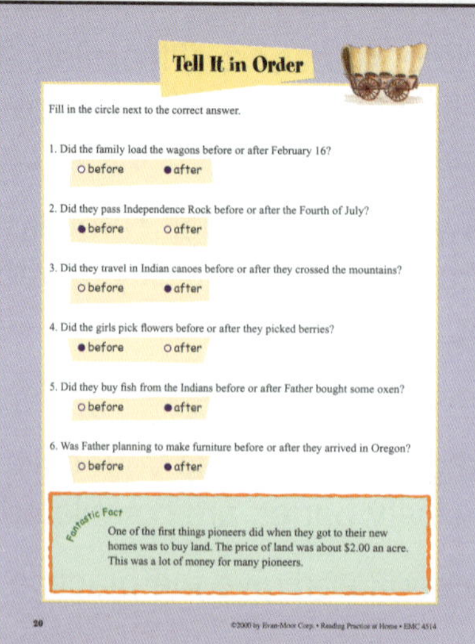

Tell It in Order

Fill in the circle next to the correct answer.

1. Did the family load the wagons before or after February 16? ○ before ● after
2. Did they pass Independence Rock before or after the Fourth of July? ● before ○ after
3. Did they travel in Indian canoes before or after they crossed the mountains? ○ before ● after
4. Did the girls pick flowers before or after they picked berries? ● before ○ after
5. Did they buy fish from the Indians before or after Father bought some oxen? ○ before ● after
6. Was Father planning to make furniture before or after they arrived in Oregon? ○ before ● after

Fantastic Fact: One of the first things pioneers did when they got to their new homes was to buy land. The price of land was about $2.00 an acre. This was a lot of money for many pioneers.

20 ©2000 by Evan-Moor Corp. • Reading Practice at Home • EMC 4514

Page 19

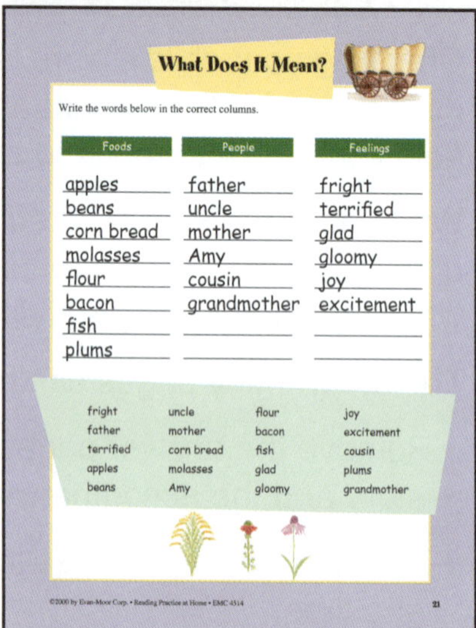

What Does It Mean?

Write the words below in the correct columns.

Foods	People	Feelings
apples	father	fright
beans	uncle	terrified
corn bread	mother	glad
molasses	Amy	gloomy
flour	cousin	joy
bacon	grandmother	excitement
fish		
plums		

fright, father, terrified, apples, beans, uncle, mother, corn bread, molasses, Amy, flour, bacon, fish, glad, gloomy, joy, excitement, cousin, plums, grandmother

©2000 by Evan-Moor Corp. • Reading Practice at Home • EMC 4514 21

Page 20

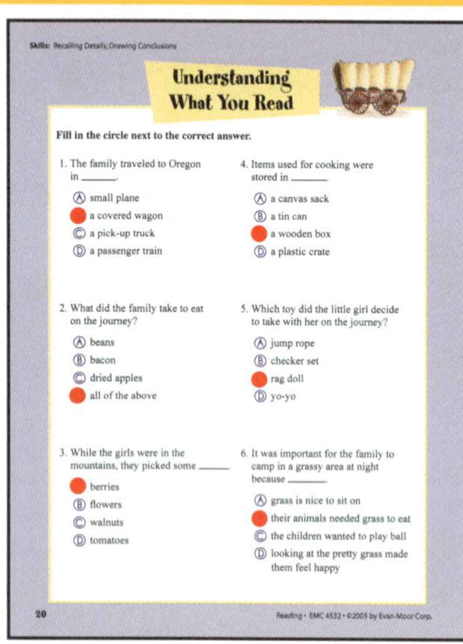

Skills: Recalling Details; Drawing Conclusions

Understanding What You Read

Fill in the circle next to the correct answer.

1. The family traveled to Oregon in ____.
   - Ⓐ small plane
   - ● a covered wagon
   - Ⓒ a pick-up truck
   - Ⓓ a passenger train
2. What did the family take to eat on the journey?
   - Ⓐ beans
   - Ⓑ bacon
   - Ⓒ dried apples
   - ● all of the above
3. While the girls were in the mountains, they picked some ____.
   - ● berries
   - Ⓑ flowers
   - Ⓒ walnuts
   - Ⓓ tomatoes
4. Items used for cooking were stored in ____.
   - Ⓐ a canvas sack
   - Ⓑ a tin can
   - ● a wooden box
   - Ⓓ a plastic crate
5. Which toy did the little girl decide to take with her on the journey?
   - Ⓐ jump rope
   - Ⓑ checker set
   - ● rag doll
   - Ⓓ yo-yo
6. It was important for the family to camp in a grassy area at night because ____.
   - Ⓐ grass is nice to sit on
   - ● their animals needed grass to eat
   - Ⓒ the children wanted to play ball
   - Ⓓ looking at the pretty grass made them feel happy

20 Reading • EMC 4532 • ©2005 by Evan-Moor Corp.

Page 21

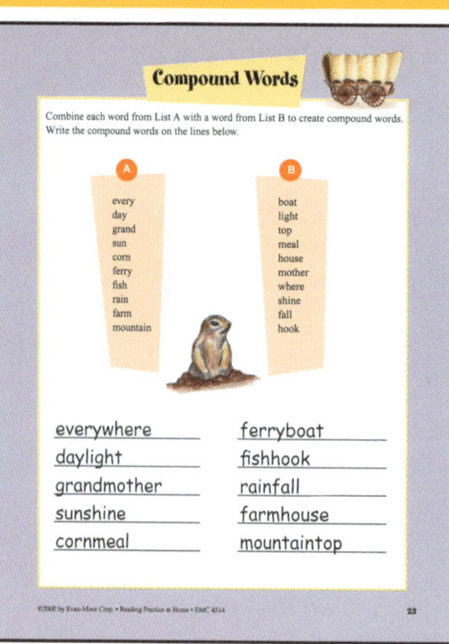

Compound Words

Combine each word from List A with a word from List B to create compound words. Write the compound words on the lines below.

A	B
every	boat
day	light
grand	top
sun	meal
corn	house
ferry	mother
fish	where
rain	shine
farm	fall
mountain	hook

everywhere	ferryboat
daylight	fishhook
grandmother	rainfall
sunshine	farmhouse
cornmeal	mountaintop

©2000 by Evan-Moor Corp. • Reading Practice at Home • EMC 4514 23

Page 22

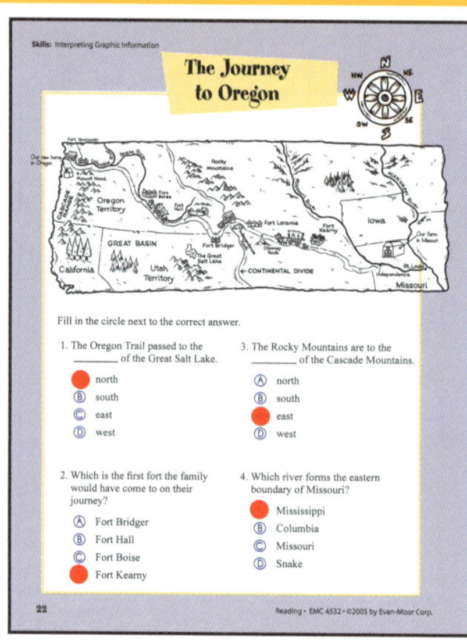

Skills: Interpreting Graphic Information

The Journey to Oregon

Fill in the circle next to the correct answer.

1. The Oregon Trail passed to the ____ of the Great Salt Lake.
   - ● north
   - Ⓑ south
   - Ⓒ east
   - Ⓓ west
2. Which is the first fort the family would have come to on their journey?
   - Ⓐ Fort Bridger
   - Ⓑ Fort Hall
   - Ⓒ Fort Boise
   - ● Fort Kearny
3. The Rocky Mountains are to the ____ of the Cascade Mountains.
   - Ⓐ north
   - Ⓑ south
   - ● east
   - Ⓓ west
4. Which river forms the eastern boundary of Missouri?
   - ● Mississippi
   - Ⓑ Columbia
   - Ⓒ Missouri
   - Ⓓ Snake

22 Reading • EMC 4532 • ©2005 by Evan-Moor Corp.

Page 24

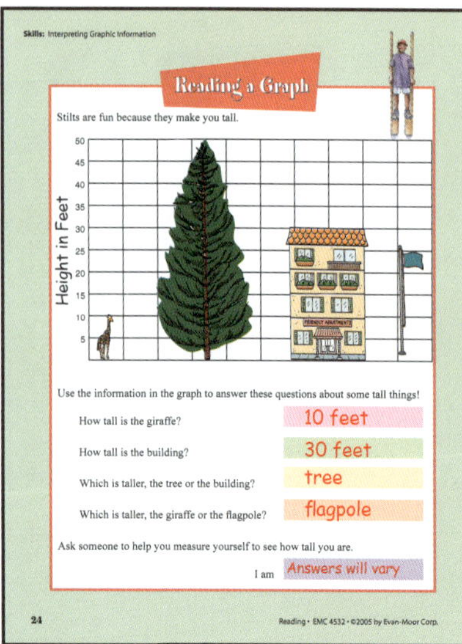

Skills: Interpreting Graphic Information

Reading a Graph

Stilts are fun because they make you tall.

Use the information in the graph to answer these questions about some tall things!

How tall is the giraffe?	10 feet
How tall is the building?	30 feet
Which is taller, the tree or the building?	tree
Which is taller, the giraffe or the flagpole?	flagpole

Ask someone to help you measure yourself to see how tall you are.

I am Answers will vary

24 Reading • EMC 4532 • ©2005 by Evan-Moor Corp.

Page 25

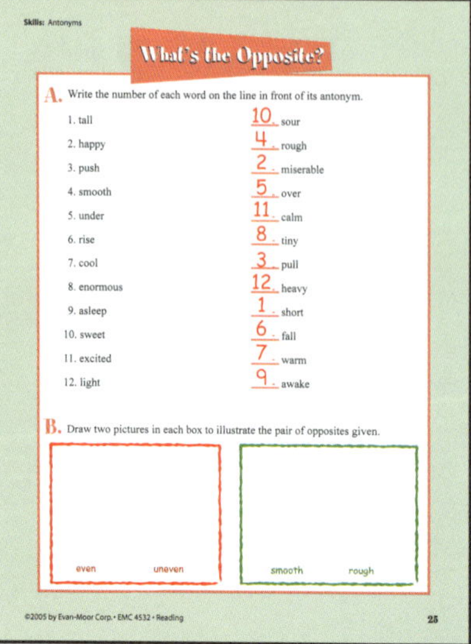

Skills: Antonyms

What's the Opposite?

A. Write the number of each word on the line in front of its antonym.

1. tall	10 sour
2. happy	4 rough
3. push	2 miserable
4. smooth	5 over
5. under	11 calm
6. rise	8 tiny
7. cool	3 pull
8. enormous	12 heavy
9. asleep	1 short
10. sweet	6 fall
11. excited	7 warm
12. light	9 awake

B. Draw two pictures in each box to illustrate the pair of opposites given.

even uneven | smooth rough

©2005 by Evan-Moor Corp. • EMC 4532 • Reading 25

Page 29

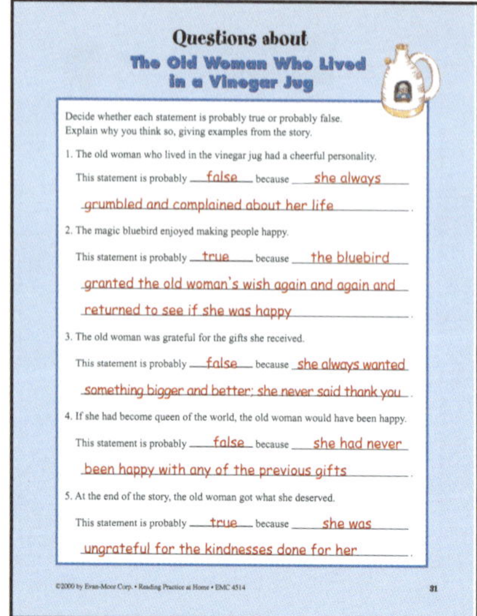

Questions about The Old Woman Who Lived in a Vinegar Jug

Decide whether each statement is probably true or probably false. Explain why you think so, giving examples from the story.

1. The old woman who lived in the vinegar jug had a cheerful personality.
   This statement is probably false because she always grumbled and complained about her life.
2. The magic bluebird enjoyed making people happy.
   This statement is probably true because the bluebird granted the old woman's wish again and again and returned to see if she was happy.
3. The old woman was grateful for the gifts she received.
   This statement is probably false because she always wanted something bigger and better; she never said thank you.
4. If she had become queen of the world, the old woman would have been happy.
   This statement is probably false because she had never been happy with any of the previous gifts.
5. At the end of the story, the old woman got what she deserved.
   This statement is probably true because she was ungrateful for the kindnesses done for her.

©2000 by Evan-Moor Corp. • Reading Practice at Home • EMC 4514 31

Page 30

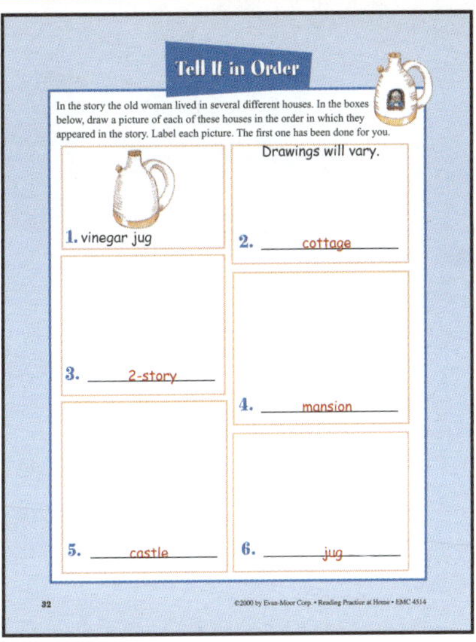

Tell It in Order

In the story the old woman lived in several different houses. In the boxes below, draw a picture of each of these houses in the order in which they appeared in the story. Label each picture. The first one has been done for you.

Drawings will vary.

1. vinegar jug
2. cottage
3. 2-story
4. mansion
5. castle
6. jug

32 ©2000 by Evan-Moor Corp. • Reading Practice at Home • EMC 4514

Page 31

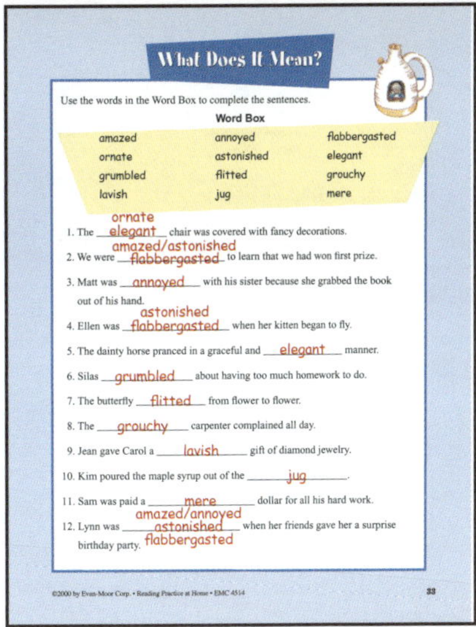

What Does It Mean?

Use the words in the Word Box to complete the sentences.

Word Box

amazed	annoyed	flabbergasted
ornate	astonished	elegant
grumbled	flitted	grouchy
lavish	jug	mere

1. The ornate / elegant chair was covered with fancy decorations.
2. We were amazed/astonished / flabbergasted to learn that we had won first prize.
3. Matt was annoyed with his sister because she grabbed the book out of his hand.
4. Ellen was astonished / flabbergasted when her kitten began to fly.
5. The dainty horse pranced in a graceful and elegant manner.
6. Silas grumbled about having too much homework to do.
7. The butterfly flitted from flower to flower.
8. The grouchy carpenter complained all day.
9. Jean gave Carol a lavish gift of diamond jewelry.
10. Kim poured the maple syrup out of the jug.
11. Sam was paid a mere dollar for all his hard work.
12. Lynn was amazed/annoyed / astonished / flabbergasted when her friends gave her a surprise birthday party.

©2000 by Evan-Moor Corp. • Reading Practice at Home • EMC 4514 33

Page 32

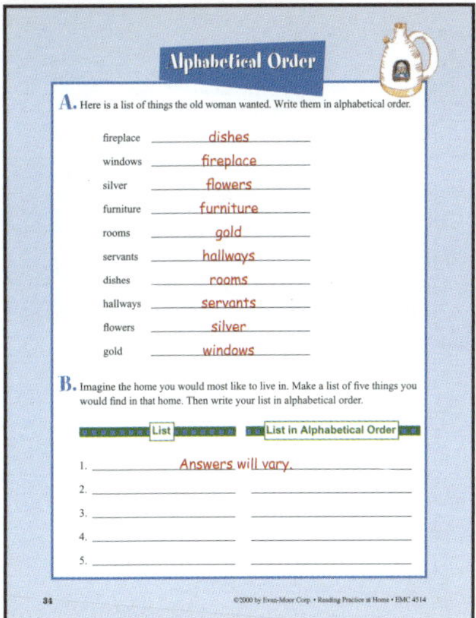

Alphabetical Order

A. Here is a list of things the old woman wanted. Write them in alphabetical order.

fireplace	dishes
windows	fireplace
silver	flowers
furniture	furniture
rooms	gold
servants	hallways
dishes	rooms
hallways	servants
flowers	silver
gold	windows

B. Imagine the home you would most like to live in. Make a list of five things you would find in that home. Then write your list in alphabetical order.

List	List in Alphabetical Order
1. Answers will vary.	
2.	
3.	
4.	
5.	

34 ©2000 by Evan-Moor Corp. • Reading Practice at Home • EMC 4514

Page 33

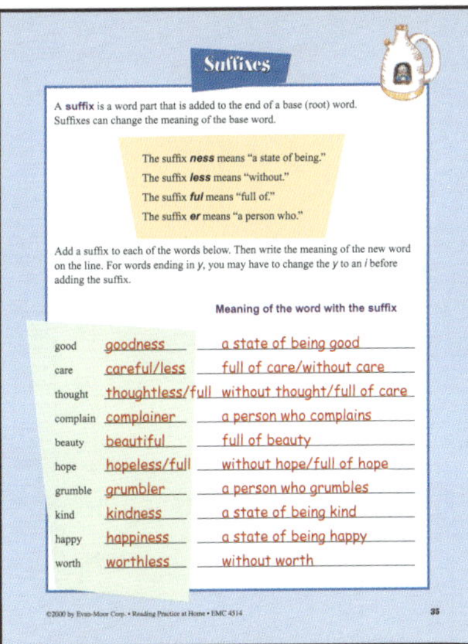

Suffixes

A **suffix** is a word part that is added to the end of a base (root) word. Suffixes can change the meaning of the base word.

The suffix ***ness*** means "a state of being."
The suffix ***less*** means "without."
The suffix ***ful*** means "full of."
The suffix ***er*** means "a person who."

Add a suffix to each of the words below. Then write the meaning of the new word on the line. For words ending in *y*, you may have to change the *y* to an *i* before adding the suffix.

		Meaning of the word with the suffix
good	goodness	a state of being good
care	careful/less	full of care/without care
thought	thoughtless/full	without thought/full of care
complain	complainer	a person who complains
beauty	beautiful	full of beauty
hope	hopeless/full	without hope/full of hope
grumble	grumbler	a person who grumbles
kind	kindness	a state of being kind
happy	happiness	a state of being happy
worth	worthless	without worth

©2000 by Evan-Moor Corp. • Reading Practice at Home • EMC 4514 35

Page 34

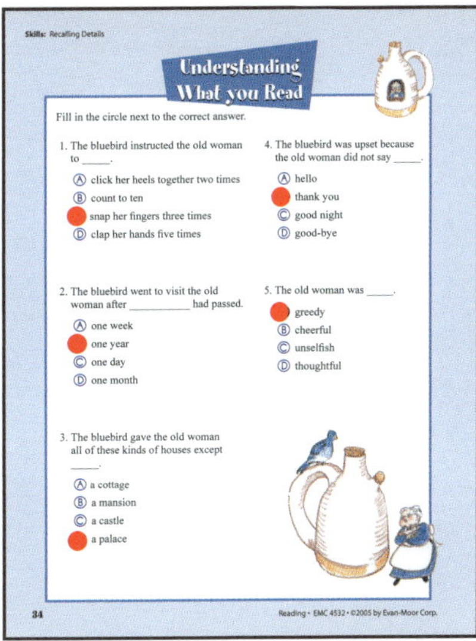

Skills: Recalling Details

Understanding What you Read

Fill in the circle next to the correct answer.

1. The bluebird instructed the old woman to ____.
   - Ⓐ click her heels together two times
   - Ⓑ count to ten
   - ● snap her fingers three times
   - Ⓓ clap her hands five times
2. The bluebird went to visit the old woman after ________ had passed.
   - Ⓐ one week
   - ● one year
   - Ⓒ one day
   - Ⓓ one month
3. The bluebird gave the old woman all of these kinds of houses except ____.
   - Ⓐ a cottage
   - Ⓑ a mansion
   - Ⓒ a castle
   - ● a palace
4. The bluebird was upset because the old woman did not say ____.
   - Ⓐ hello
   - ● thank you
   - Ⓒ good night
   - Ⓓ good-bye
5. The old woman was ____.
   - ● greedy
   - Ⓑ cheerful
   - Ⓒ unselfish
   - Ⓓ thoughtful

34 Reading • EMC 4532 • ©2005 by Evan-Moor Corp.

Page 42

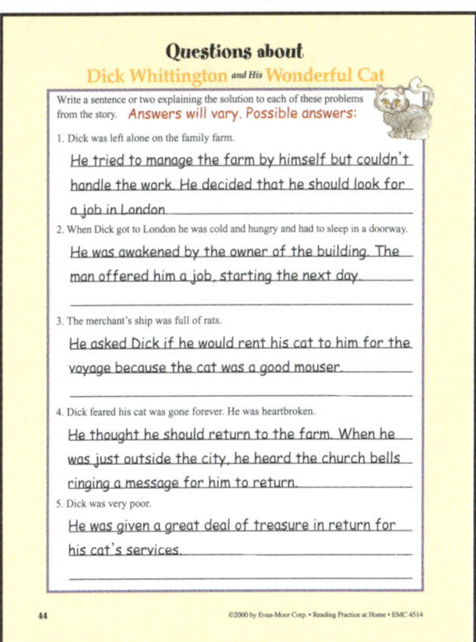

Questions about Dick Whittington and His Wonderful Cat

Write a sentence or two explaining the solution to each of these problems from the story. Answers will vary. Possible answers:

1. Dick was left alone on the family farm.
   He tried to manage the farm by himself but couldn't handle the work. He decided that he should look for a job in London.
2. When Dick got to London he was cold and hungry and had to sleep in a doorway.
   He was awakened by the owner of the building. The man offered him a job, starting the next day.
3. The merchant's ship was full of rats.
   He asked Dick if he would rent his cat to him for the voyage because the cat was a good mouser.
4. Dick feared his cat was gone forever. He was heartbroken.
   He thought he should return to the farm. When he was just outside the city, he heard the church bells ringing a message for him to return.
5. Dick was very poor.
   He was given a great deal of treasure in return for his cat's services.

44 ©2000 by Evan-Moor Corp. • Reading Practice at Home • EMC 4514

Page 43

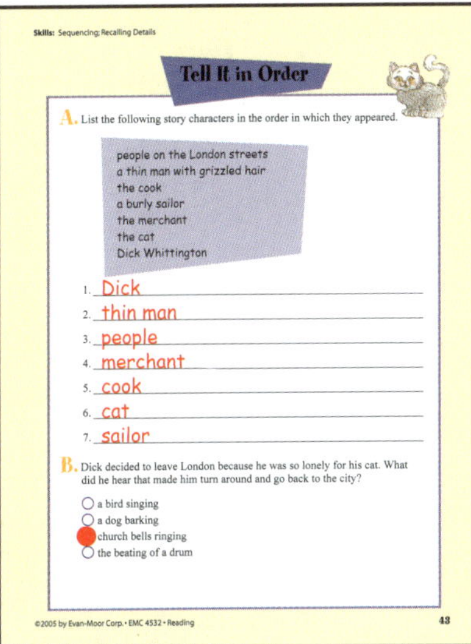

Skills: Sequencing; Recalling Details

Tell It in Order

A. List the following story characters in the order in which they appeared.

people on the London streets
a thin man with grizzled hair
the cook
a burly sailor
the merchant
the cat
Dick Whittington

1. Dick
2. thin man
3. people
4. merchant
5. cook
6. cat
7. sailor

B. Dick decided to leave London because he was so lonely for his cat. What did he hear that made him turn around and go back to the city?

- ○ a bird singing
- ○ a dog barking
- ● church bells ringing
- ○ the beating of a drum

©2005 by Evan-Moor Corp. • EMC 4532 • Reading 43

Page 44

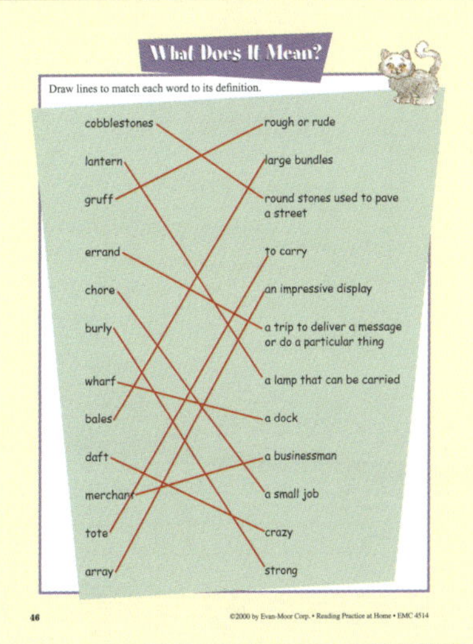

What Does It Mean?

Draw lines to match each word to its definition.

cobblestones	rough or rude
lantern	large bundles
gruff	round stones used to pave a street
errand	to carry
chore	an impressive display
burly	a trip to deliver a message or do a particular thing
wharf	a lamp that can be carried
bales	a dock
daft	a businessman
merchant	a small job
tote	crazy
array	strong

46 ©2000 by Evan-Moor Corp. • Reading Practice at Home • EMC 4514

Page 45

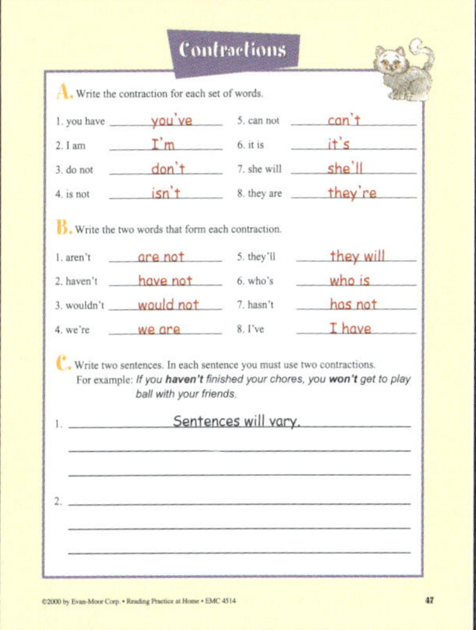

Contractions

A. Write the contraction for each set of words.

1. you have	you've	5. can not	can't
2. I am	I'm	6. it is	it's
3. do not	don't	7. she will	she'll
4. is not	isn't	8. they are	they're

B. Write the two words that form each contraction.

1. aren't	are not	5. they'll	they will
2. haven't	have not	6. who's	who is
3. wouldn't	would not	7. hasn't	has not
4. we're	we are	8. I've	I have

C. Write two sentences. In each sentence you must use two contractions.
For example: *If you **haven't** finished your chores, you **won't** get to play ball with your friends.*

1. Sentences will vary.
2.

©2000 by Evan-Moor Corp. • Reading Practice at Home • EMC 4514 47

Page 46

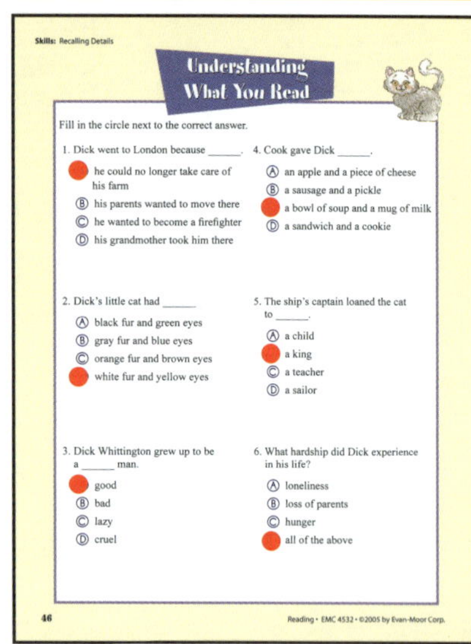

Skill: Recalling Details

Understanding What You Read

Fill in the circle next to the correct answer.

1. Dick went to London because ______.
   - ● he could no longer take care of his farm
   - Ⓑ his parents wanted to move there
   - Ⓒ he wanted to become a firefighter
   - Ⓓ his grandmother took him there
2. Dick's little cat had ______.
   - Ⓐ black fur and green eyes
   - Ⓑ gray fur and blue eyes
   - Ⓒ orange fur and brown eyes
   - ● white fur and yellow eyes
3. Dick Whittington grew up to be a ______ man.
   - ● good
   - Ⓑ bad
   - Ⓒ lazy
   - Ⓓ cruel
4. Cook gave Dick ______.
   - Ⓐ an apple and a piece of cheese
   - Ⓑ a sausage and a pickle
   - ● a bowl of soup and a mug of milk
   - Ⓓ a sandwich and a cookie
5. The ship's captain loaned the cat to ______.
   - Ⓐ a child
   - ● a king
   - Ⓒ a teacher
   - Ⓓ a sailor
6. What hardship did Dick experience in his life?
   - Ⓐ loneliness
   - Ⓑ loss of parents
   - Ⓒ hunger
   - ● all of the above

46 Reading • EMC 4532 • ©2005 by Evan-Moor Corp.

Page 47

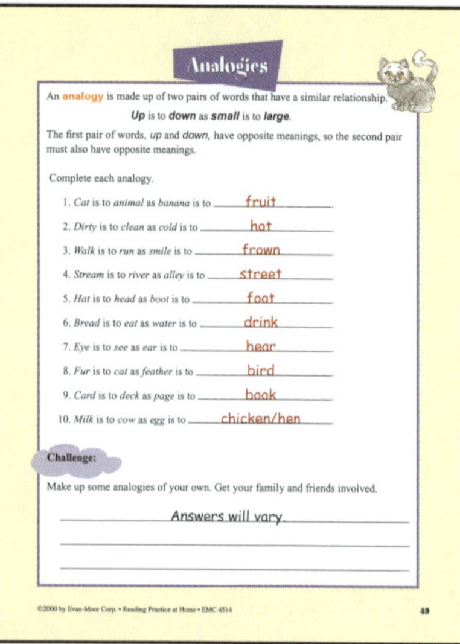

Analogies

An **analogy** is made up of two pairs of words that have a similar relationship.

Up is to *down* as *small* is to *large*.

The first pair of words, *up* and *down*, have opposite meanings, so the second pair must also have opposite meanings.

Complete each analogy.

1. *Cat* is to *animal* as *banana* is to fruit
2. *Dirty* is to *clean* as *cold* is to hot
3. *Walk* is to *run* as *smile* is to frown
4. *Stream* is to *river* as *alley* is to street
5. *Hat* is to *head* as *boot* is to foot
6. *Bread* is to *eat* as *water* is to drink
7. *Eye* is to *see* as *ear* is to hear
8. *Fur* is to *cat* as *feather* is to bird
9. *Card* is to *deck* as *page* is to book
10. *Milk* is to *cow* as *egg* is to chicken/hen

Challenge:

Make up some analogies of your own. Get your family and friends involved.

Answers will vary.

©2000 by Evan-Moor Corp. • Reading Practice at Home • EMC 4514 49

Page 51

Skill: Recalling Details

Questions about Go Fly a Kite

1. Name three ways people have used kites.

   Kites have been used in war as targets and to carry cameras. Kites have carried radio equipment to send and receive signals. Kites have been used for fun.

2. Why did Benjamin Franklin fly a kite?

   He wanted to prove that lightning was a form of electricity.

3. You should never fly a kite ______.
   - ○ on a hill
   - ● during a storm
   - ○ in the morning
   - ○ by yourself

4. Why is Kites' Day celebrated in China?

   Kite day is celebrated because a legend tells of a family that was saved from disaster because they were out flying kites. If people fly kites that day it will bring them good luck.

5. The windsocks flown in Japan on Children's Day are shaped like what animal? Why?

   They are shaped like a carp, which stands for the strength, hard work, and courage needed to succeed in life.

51 Reading • EMC 4532 • ©2005 by Evan-Moor Corp.

Page 52

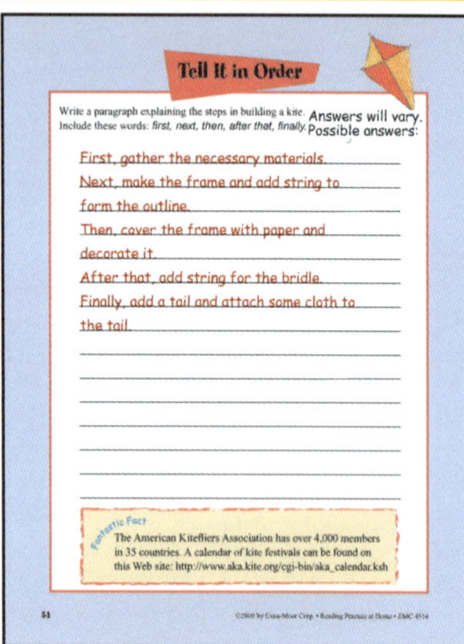

Tell It in Order

Write a paragraph explaining the steps in building a kite. Include these words: *first, next, then, after that, finally.* Answers will vary. Possible answers:

First, gather the necessary materials. Next, make the frame and add string to form the outline. Then, cover the frame with paper and decorate it. After that, add string for the bridle. Finally, add a tail and attach some cloth to the tail.

Fantastic Fact: The American Kitefliers Association has over 4,000 members in 35 countries. A calendar of kite festivals can be found on this Web site: http://www.aka.kite.org/cgi-bin/aka_calendar.ksh

54 ©2000 by Evan-Moor Corp. • Reading Practice at Home • EMC 4514

Page 53

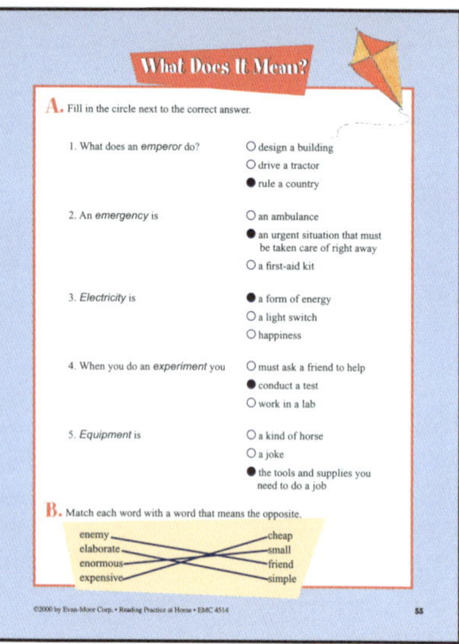

What Does It Mean?

A. Fill in the circle next to the correct answer.

1. What does an *emperor* do?
   - ○ design a building
   - ○ drive a tractor
   - ● rule a country
2. An *emergency* is
   - ○ an ambulance
   - ● an urgent situation that must be taken care of right away
   - ○ a first-aid kit
3. *Electricity* is
   - ● a form of energy
   - ○ a light switch
   - ○ happiness
4. When you do an *experiment* you
   - ○ must ask a friend to help
   - ● conduct a test
   - ○ work in a lab
5. *Equipment* is
   - ○ a kind of horse
   - ○ a joke
   - ● the tools and supplies you need to do a job

B. Match each word with a word that means the opposite.

enemy — friend
elaborate — simple
enormous — small
expensive — cheap

©2000 by Evan-Moor Corp. • Reading Practice at Home • EMC 4514 55

Page 54

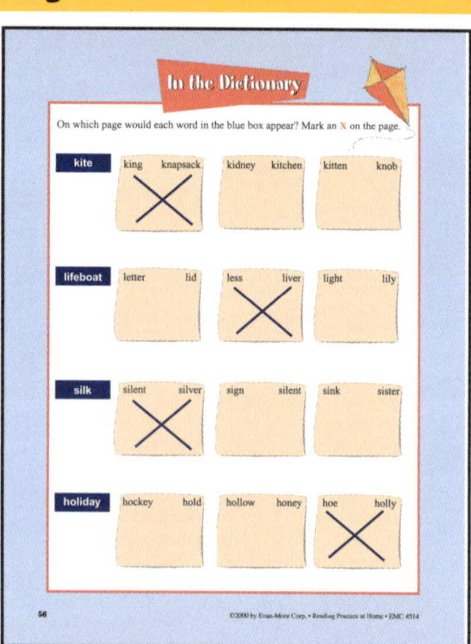

In the Dictionary

On which page would each word in the blue box appear? Mark an X on the page.

Word	king – knapsack	kidney – kitchen	kitten – knob
kite	X		

Word	letter – lid	less – liver	light – lily
lifeboat		X	

Word	silent – silver	sign – silent	sink – sister
silk	X		

Word	hockey – hold	hollow – honey	hoe – holly
holiday			X

56 ©2000 by Evan-Moor Corp. • Reading Practice at Home • EMC 4514

Page 55

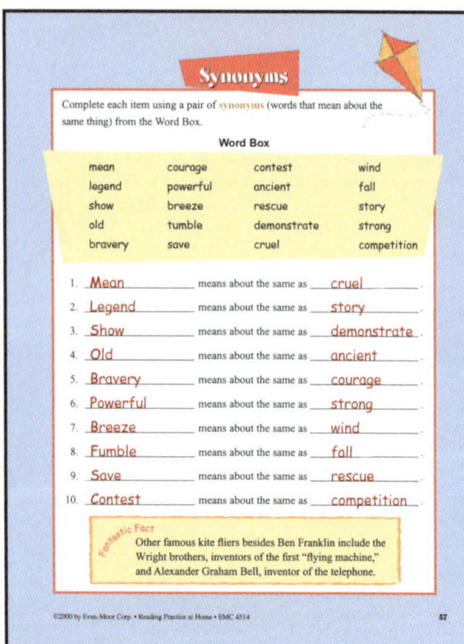

Synonyms

Complete each item using a pair of synonyms (words that mean about the same thing) from the Word Box.

Word Box

mean	courage	contest	wind
legend	powerful	ancient	fall
show	breeze	rescue	story
old	tumble	demonstrate	strong
bravery	save	cruel	competition

1. Mean means about the same as cruel
2. Legend means about the same as story
3. Show means about the same as demonstrate
4. Old means about the same as ancient
5. Bravery means about the same as courage
6. Powerful means about the same as strong
7. Breeze means about the same as wind
8. Tumble means about the same as fall
9. Save means about the same as rescue
10. Contest means about the same as competition

Fantastic Fact: Other famous kite fliers besides Ben Franklin include the Wright brothers, inventors of the first "flying machine," and Alexander Graham Bell, inventor of the telephone.

©2000 by Evan-Moor Corp. • Reading Practice at Home • EMC 4514 57

Page 56

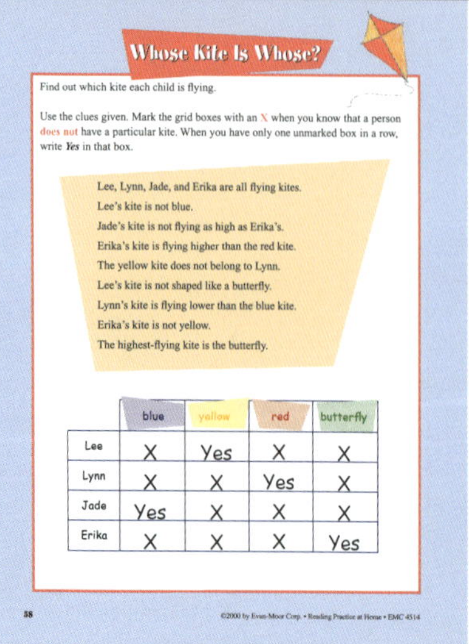

Whose Kite Is Whose?

Find out which kite each child is flying.

Use the clues given. Mark the grid boxes with an X when you know that a person does not have a particular kite. When you have only one unmarked box in a row, write *Yes* in that box.

Lee, Lynn, Jade, and Erika are all flying kites.
Lee's kite is not blue.
Jade's kite is not flying as high as Erika's.
Erika's kite is flying higher than the red kite.
The yellow kite does not belong to Lynn.
Lee's kite is not shaped like a butterfly.
Lynn's kite is flying lower than the blue kite.
Erika's kite is not yellow.
The highest-flying kite is the butterfly.

	blue	yellow	red	butterfly
Lee	X	Yes	X	X
Lynn	X	X	Yes	X
Jade	Yes	X	X	X
Erika	X	X	X	Yes

58 ©2000 by Evan-Moor Corp. • Reading Practice at Home • EMC 4514

Page 58

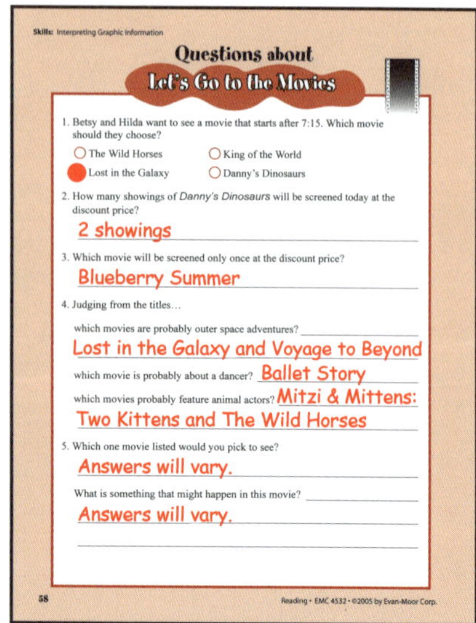

Skill: Interpreting Graphic Information

Questions about Let's Go to the Movies

1. Betsy and Hilda want to see a movie that starts after 7:15. Which movie should they choose?
   - ○ The Wild Horses
   - ○ King of the World
   - ● Lost in the Galaxy
   - ○ Danny's Dinosaurs
2. How many showings of *Danny's Dinosaurs* will be screened today at the discount price?

   2 showings

3. Which movie will be screened only once at the discount price?

   Blueberry Summer

4. Judging from the titles...

   which movies are probably outer space adventures? Lost in the Galaxy and Voyage to Beyond

   which movie is probably about a dancer? Ballet Story

   which movies probably feature animal actors? Mitzi & Mittens; Two Kittens and The Wild Horses

5. Which one movie listed would you pick to see?

   Answers will vary.

   What is something that might happen in this movie?

   Answers will vary.

58 Reading • EMC 4532 • ©2005 by Evan-Moor Corp.

Page 59

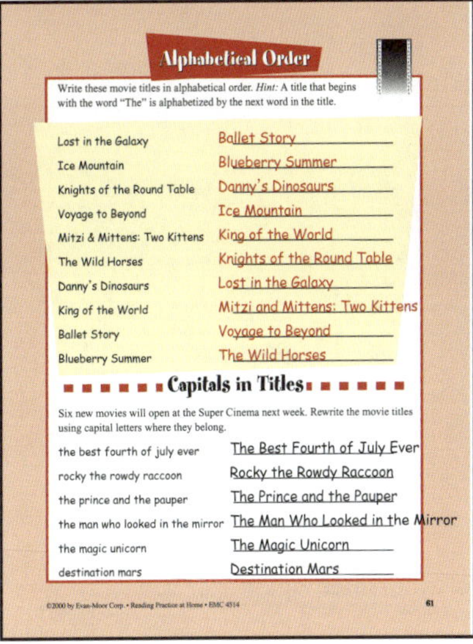

Alphabetical Order

Write these movie titles in alphabetical order. *Hint:* A title that begins with the word "The" is alphabetized by the next word in the title.

Lost in the Galaxy	Ballet Story
Ice Mountain	Blueberry Summer
Knights of the Round Table	Danny's Dinosaurs
Voyage to Beyond	Ice Mountain
Mitzi & Mittens: Two Kittens	King of the World
The Wild Horses	Knights of the Round Table
Danny's Dinosaurs	Lost in the Galaxy
King of the World	Mitzi and Mittens: Two Kittens
Ballet Story	Voyage to Beyond
Blueberry Summer	The Wild Horses

Capitals in Titles

Six new movies will open at the Super Cinema next week. Rewrite the movie titles using capital letters where they belong.

the best fourth of july ever	The Best Fourth of July Ever
rocky the rowdy raccoon	Rocky the Rowdy Raccoon
the prince and the pauper	The Prince and the Pauper
the man who looked in the mirror	The Man Who Looked in the Mirror
the magic unicorn	The Magic Unicorn
destination mars	Destination Mars

©2000 by Evan-Moor Corp. • Reading Practice at Home • EMC 4514 61

Page 65

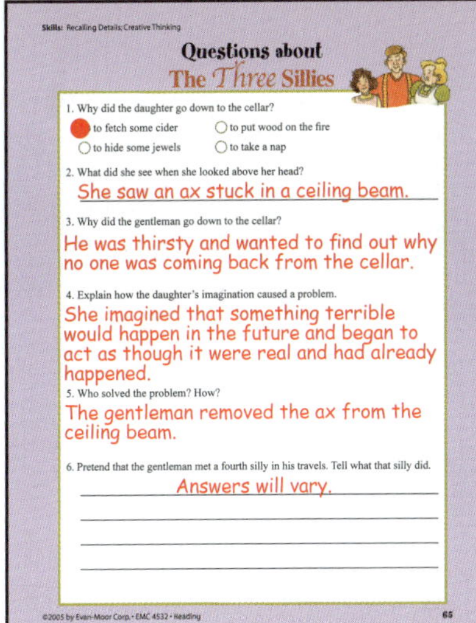

Skills: Recalling Details; Creative Thinking

Questions about The Three Sillies

1. Why did the daughter go down to the cellar?
   - ● to fetch some cider
   - ○ to put wood on the fire
   - ○ to hide some jewels
   - ○ to take a nap
2. What did she see when she looked above her head?
   She saw an ax stuck in a ceiling beam.
3. Why did the gentleman go down to the cellar?
   He was thirsty and wanted to find out why no one was coming back from the cellar.
4. Explain how the daughter's imagination caused a problem.
   She imagined that something terrible would happen in the future and began to act as though it were real and had already happened.
5. Who solved the problem? How?
   The gentleman removed the ax from the ceiling beam.
6. Pretend that the gentleman met a fourth silly in his travels. Tell what that silly did.
   Answers will vary.

©2005 by Evan-Moor Corp. • EMC 4532 • Reading 65

Page 66

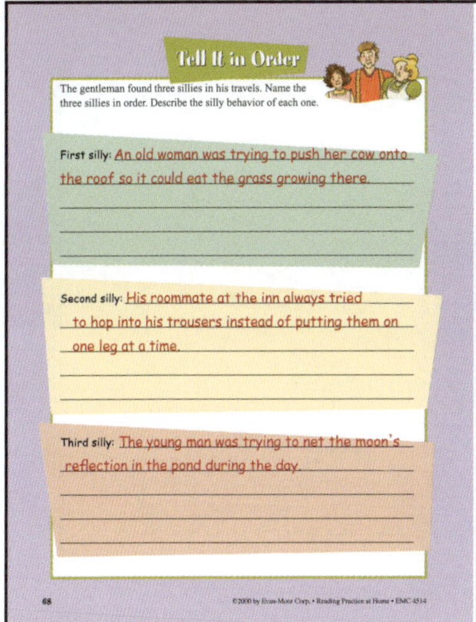

Tell It in Order

The gentleman found three sillies in his travels. Name the three sillies in order. Describe the silly behavior of each one.

First silly: An old woman was trying to push her cow onto the roof so it could eat the grass growing there.

Second silly: His roommate at the inn always tried to hop into his trousers instead of putting them on one leg at a time.

Third silly: The young man was trying to net the moon's reflection in the pond during the day.

68 ©2000 by Evan-Moor Corp. • Reading Practice at Home • EMC 4514

Page 67

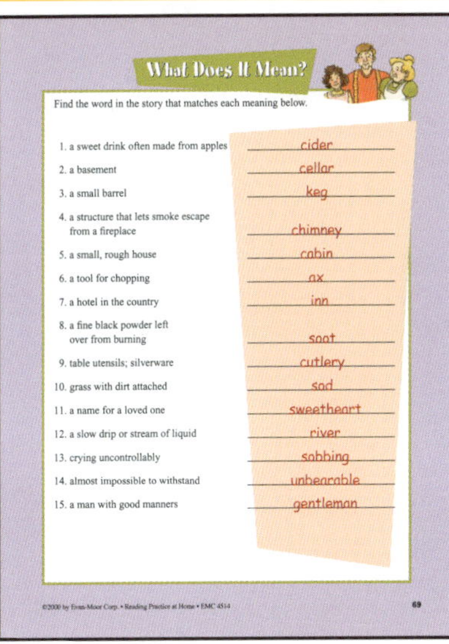

What Does It Mean?

Find the word in the story that matches each meaning below.

1. a sweet drink often made from apples — cider
2. a basement — cellar
3. a small barrel — keg
4. a structure that lets smoke escape from a fireplace — chimney
5. a small, rough house — cabin
6. a tool for chopping — ax
7. a hotel in the country — inn
8. a fine black powder left over from burning — soot
9. table utensils; silverware — cutlery
10. grass with dirt attached — sod
11. a name for a loved one — sweetheart
12. a slow drip or stream of liquid — river
13. crying uncontrollably — sobbing
14. almost impossible to withstand — unbearable
15. a man with good manners — gentleman

©2000 by Evan-Moor Corp. • Reading Practice at Home • EMC 4514 69

Page 68

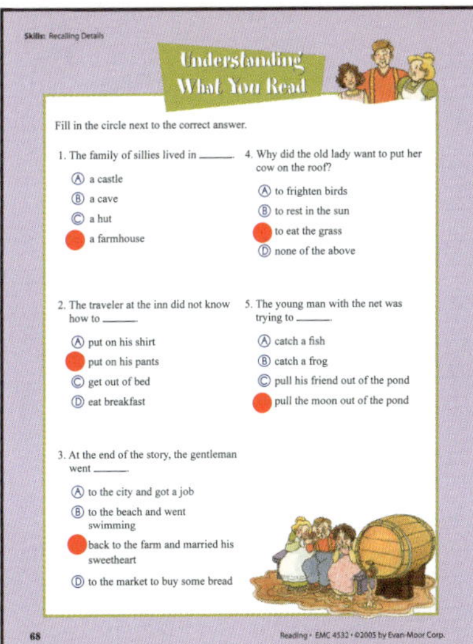

Skills: Recalling Details

Understanding What You Read

Fill in the circle next to the correct answer.

1. The family of sillies lived in ____.
   - Ⓐ a castle
   - Ⓑ a cave
   - Ⓒ a hut
   - ● a farmhouse
2. The traveler at the inn did not know how to ____.
   - Ⓐ put on his shirt
   - ● put on his pants
   - Ⓒ get out of bed
   - Ⓓ eat breakfast
3. At the end of the story, the gentleman went ____.
   - Ⓐ to the city and got a job
   - Ⓑ to the beach and went swimming
   - ● back to the farm and married his sweetheart
   - Ⓓ to the market to buy some bread
4. Why did the old lady want to put her cow on the roof?
   - Ⓐ to frighten birds
   - Ⓑ to rest in the sun
   - ● to eat the grass
   - Ⓓ none of the above
5. The young man with the net was trying to ____.
   - Ⓐ catch a fish
   - Ⓑ catch a frog
   - Ⓒ pull his friend out of the pond
   - ● pull the moon out of the pond

68 Reading • EMC 4532 • ©2005 by Evan-Moor Corp.

Page 69

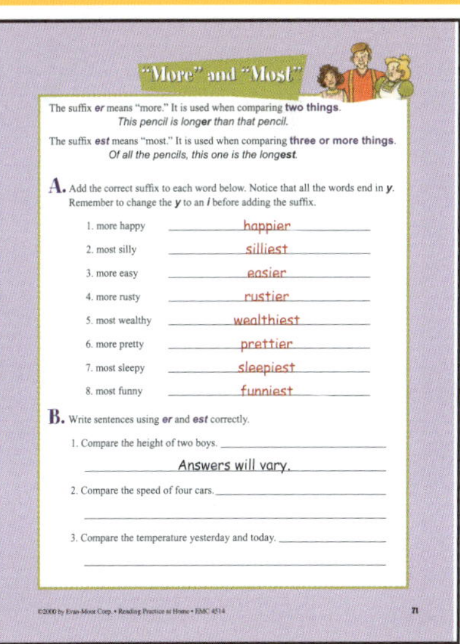

"More" and "Most"

The suffix **er** means "more." It is used when comparing **two things**.
This pencil is longer than that pencil.

The suffix **est** means "most." It is used when comparing **three or more things**.
Of all the pencils, this one is the longest.

A. Add the correct suffix to each word below. Notice that all the words end in **y**. Remember to change the **y** to an **i** before adding the suffix.

1. more happy — happier
2. most silly — silliest
3. more easy — easier
4. more rusty — rustier
5. most wealthy — wealthiest
6. more pretty — prettier
7. most sleepy — sleepiest
8. most funny — funniest

B. Write sentences using **er** and **est** correctly.

1. Compare the height of two boys.
   Answers will vary.
2. Compare the speed of four cars.
3. Compare the temperature yesterday and today.

©2000 by Evan-Moor Corp. • Reading Practice at Home • EMC 4514 71

Page 70

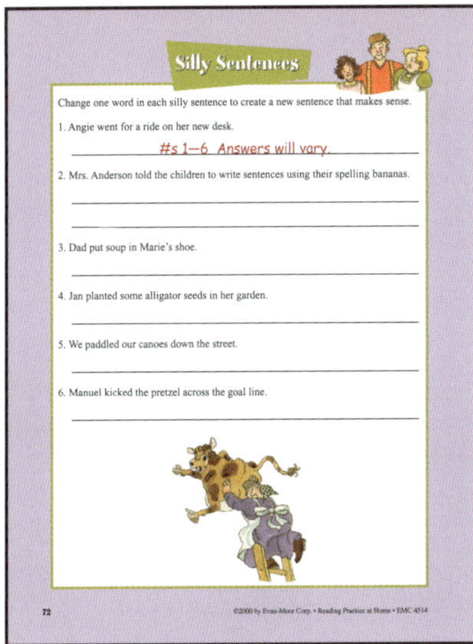

Silly Sentences

Change one word in each silly sentence to create a new sentence that makes sense.

1. Angie went for a ride on her new desk.
   #s 1–6 Answers will vary.
2. Mrs. Anderson told the children to write sentences using their spelling bananas.
3. Dad put soup in Marie's shoe.
4. Jan planted some alligator seeds in her garden.
5. We paddled our canoes down the street.
6. Manuel kicked the pretzel across the goal line.

72 ©2000 by Evan-Moor Corp. • Reading Practice at Home • EMC 4514

Page 75

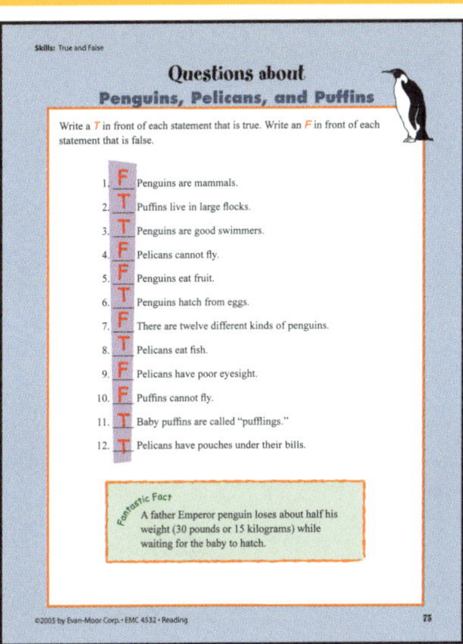

Skills: True and False

Questions about Penguins, Pelicans, and Puffins

Write a *T* in front of each statement that is true. Write an *F* in front of each statement that is false.

1. F Penguins are mammals.
2. T Puffins live in large flocks.
3. T Penguins are good swimmers.
4. F Pelicans cannot fly.
5. F Penguins eat fruit.
6. T Penguins hatch from eggs.
7. F There are twelve different kinds of penguins.
8. F Pelicans eat fish.
9. F Pelicans have poor eyesight.
10. F Puffins cannot fly.
11. T Baby puffins are called "pufflings."
12. T Pelicans have pouches under their bills.

Fantastic Fact: A father Emperor penguin loses about half his weight (30 pounds or 15 kilograms) while waiting for the baby to hatch.

©2005 by Evan-Moor Corp. • EMC 4532 • Reading 75

Page 76

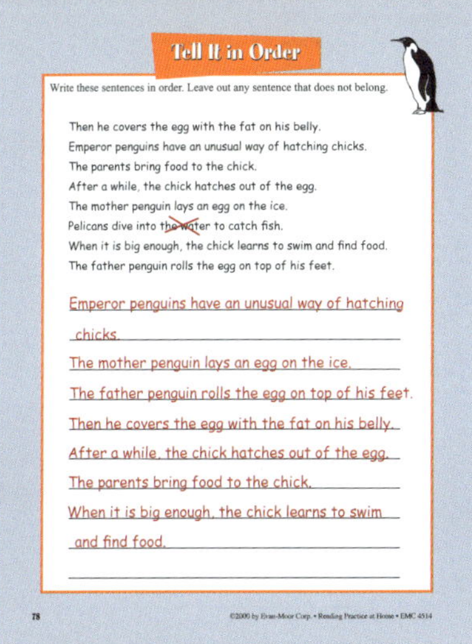

Tell It in Order

Write these sentences in order. Leave out any sentence that does not belong.

Then he covers the egg with the fat on his belly.
Emperor penguins have an unusual way of hatching chicks.
The parents bring food to the chick.
After a while, the chick hatches out of the egg.
The mother penguin lays an egg on the ice.
~~Pelicans dive into the water to catch fish.~~
When it is big enough, the chick learns to swim and find food.
The father penguin rolls the egg on top of his feet.

Emperor penguins have an unusual way of hatching chicks.
The mother penguin lays an egg on the ice.
The father penguin rolls the egg on top of his feet.
Then he covers the egg with the fat on his belly.
After a while, the chick hatches out of the egg.
The parents bring food to the chick.
When it is big enough, the chick learns to swim and find food.

78 ©2000 by Evan-Moor Corp. • Reading Practice at Home • EMC 4514

Page 77

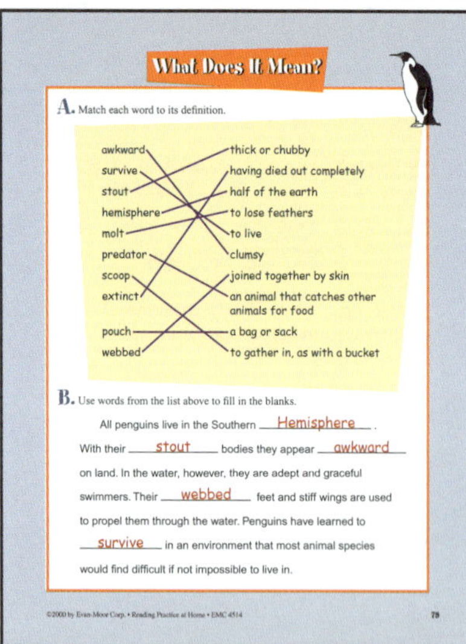

What Does It Mean?

A. Match each word to its definition.

awkward — clumsy
survive — to live
stout — thick or chubby
hemisphere — half of the earth
molt — to lose feathers
predator — an animal that catches other animals for food
scoop — to gather in, as with a bucket
extinct — having died out completely
pouch — a bag or sack
webbed — joined together by skin

B. Use words from the list above to fill in the blanks.

All penguins live in the Southern Hemisphere. With their stout bodies they appear awkward on land. In the water, however, they are adept and graceful swimmers. Their webbed feet and stiff wings are used to propel them through the water. Penguins have learned to survive in an environment that most animal species would find difficult if not impossible to live in.

Page 78

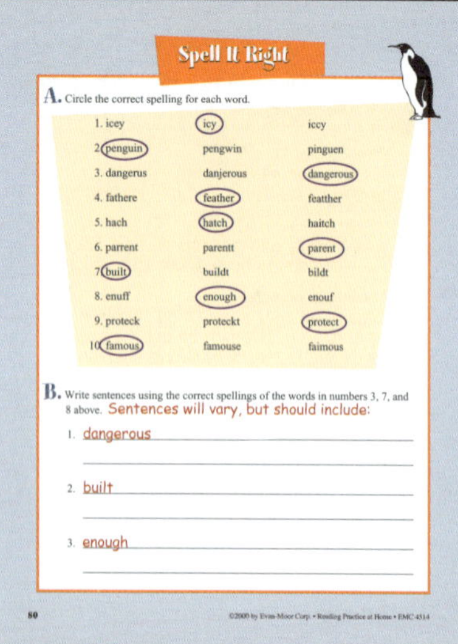

Spell It Right

A. Circle the correct spelling for each word.

1. icey — (icy) — iccy
2. (penguin) — pengwin — pinguen
3. dangerus — danjerous — (dangerous)
4. fathere — (feather) — feathter
5. hach — (hatch) — haitch
6. parrent — parentt — (parent)
7. (built) — buildt — bildt
8. enuff — (enough) — enouf
9. proteck — protectt — (protect)
10. (famous) — famouse — faimous

B. Write sentences using the correct spellings of the words in numbers 3, 7, and 8 above. Sentences will vary, but should include:

1. dangerous
2. built
3. enough

Page 79

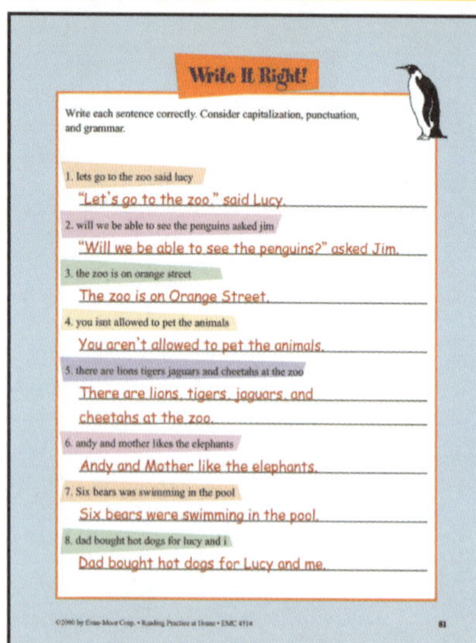

Write It Right!

Write each sentence correctly. Consider capitalization, punctuation, and grammar.

1. lets go to the zoo said lucy
"Let's go to the zoo," said Lucy.
2. will we be able to see the penguins asked jim
"Will we be able to see the penguins?" asked Jim.
3. the zoo is on orange street
The zoo is on Orange Street.
4. you isnt allowed to pet the animals
You aren't allowed to pet the animals.
5. there are lions tigers jaguars and cheetahs at the zoo
There are lions, tigers, jaguars, and cheetahs at the zoo.
6. andy and mother likes the elephants
Andy and Mother like the elephants.
7. Six bears was swimming in the pool
Six bears were swimming in the pool.
8. dad bought hot dogs for lucy and i
Dad bought hot dogs for Lucy and me.

Page 80

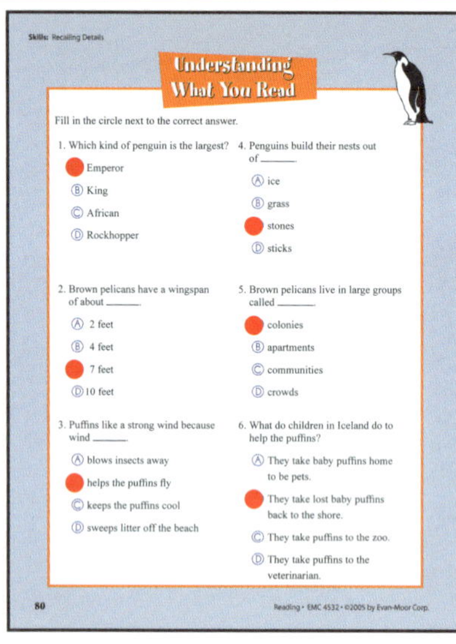

Skills: Recalling Details

Understanding What You Read

Fill in the circle next to the correct answer.

1. Which kind of penguin is the largest?
   - ● Emperor
   - Ⓑ King
   - Ⓒ African
   - Ⓓ Rockhopper
2. Brown pelicans have a wingspan of about ____.
   - Ⓐ 2 feet
   - Ⓑ 4 feet
   - ● 7 feet
   - Ⓓ 10 feet
3. Puffins like a strong wind because wind ____.
   - Ⓐ blows insects away
   - ● helps the puffins fly
   - Ⓒ keeps the puffins cool
   - Ⓓ sweeps litter off the beach
4. Penguins build their nests out of ____.
   - Ⓐ ice
   - Ⓑ grass
   - ● stones
   - Ⓓ sticks
5. Brown pelicans live in large groups called ____.
   - ● colonies
   - Ⓑ apartments
   - Ⓒ communities
   - Ⓓ crowds
6. What do children in Iceland do to help the puffins?
   - Ⓐ They take baby puffins home to be pets.
   - ● They take lost baby puffins back to the shore.
   - Ⓒ They take puffins to the zoo.
   - Ⓓ They take puffins to the veterinarian.

Page 82

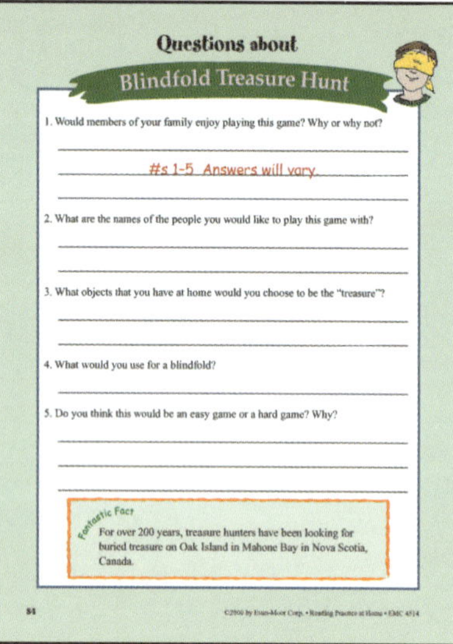

Questions about Blindfold Treasure Hunt

1. Would members of your family enjoy playing this game? Why or why not?
#s 1–5 Answers will vary.
2. What are the names of the people you would like to play this game with?
3. What objects that you have at home would you choose to be the "treasure"?
4. What would you use for a blindfold?
5. Do you think this would be an easy game or a hard game? Why?

Fantastic Fact: For over 200 years, treasure hunters have been looking for buried treasure on Oak Island in Mahone Bay in Nova Scotia, Canada.

Page 83

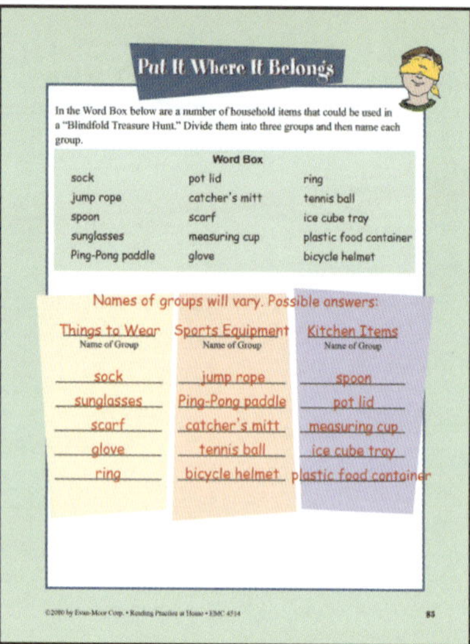

Put It Where It Belongs

In the Word Box below are a number of household items that could be used in a "Blindfold Treasure Hunt." Divide them into three groups and then name each group.

Word Box

sock	pot lid	ring
jump rope	catcher's mitt	tennis ball
spoon	scarf	ice cube tray
sunglasses	measuring cup	plastic food container
Ping-Pong paddle	glove	bicycle helmet

Names of groups will vary. Possible answers:

Things to Wear	Sports Equipment	Kitchen Items
sock	jump rope	spoon
sunglasses	Ping-Pong paddle	pot lid
scarf	catcher's mitt	measuring cup
glove	tennis ball	ice cube tray
ring	bicycle helmet	plastic food container

Page 88

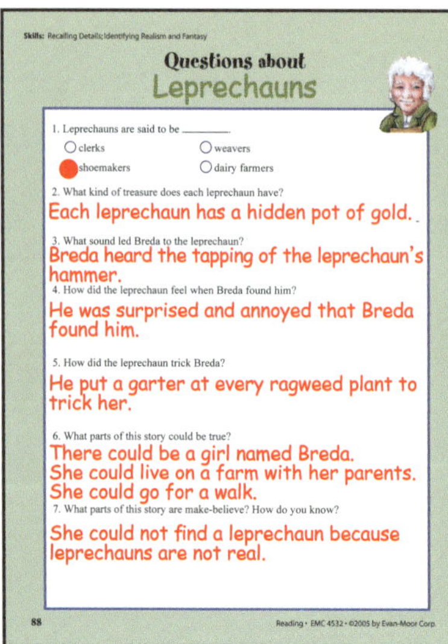

Skills: Recalling Details; Identifying Realism and Fantasy

Questions about Leprechauns

1. Leprechauns are said to be ____.
   - ○ clerks
   - ● shoemakers
   - ○ weavers
   - ○ dairy farmers
2. What kind of treasure does each leprechaun have?
Each leprechaun has a hidden pot of gold.
3. What sound led Breda to the leprechaun?
Breda heard the tapping of the leprechaun's hammer.
4. How did the leprechaun feel when Breda found him?
He was surprised and annoyed that Breda found him.
5. How did the leprechaun trick Breda?
He put a garter at every ragweed plant to trick her.
6. What parts of this story could be true?
There could be a girl named Breda. She could live on a farm with her parents. She could go for a walk.
7. What parts of this story are make-believe? How do you know?
She could not find a leprechaun because leprechauns are not real.

Page 89

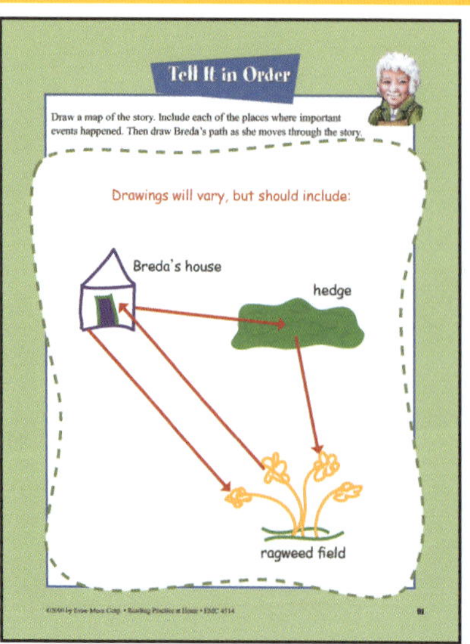

Tell It in Order

Draw a map of the story. Include each of the places where important events happened. Then draw Breda's path as she moves through the story.

Drawings will vary, but should include:

Page 90

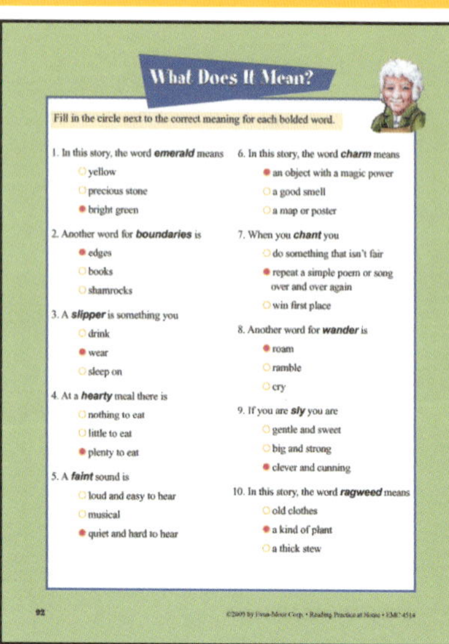

What Does It Mean?

Fill in the circle next to the correct meaning for each bolded word.

1. In this story, the word **emerald** means
   - ○ yellow
   - ○ precious stone
   - ● bright green
2. Another word for **boundaries** is
   - ● edges
   - ○ books
   - ○ shamrocks
3. A **slipper** is something you
   - ○ drink
   - ● wear
   - ○ sleep on
4. At a **hearty** meal there is
   - ○ nothing to eat
   - ○ little to eat
   - ● plenty to eat
5. A **faint** sound is
   - ○ loud and easy to hear
   - ○ musical
   - ● quiet and hard to hear
6. In this story, the word **charm** means
   - ● an object with a magic power
   - ○ a good smell
   - ○ a map or poster
7. When you **chant** you
   - ○ do something that isn't fair
   - ● repeat a simple poem or song over and over again
   - ○ win first place
8. Another word for **wander** is
   - ● roam
   - ○ ramble
   - ○ cry
9. If you are **sly** you are
   - ○ gentle and sweet
   - ○ big and strong
   - ● clever and cunning
10. In this story, the word **ragweed** means
   - ○ old clothes
   - ● a kind of plant
   - ○ a thick stew

Page 91

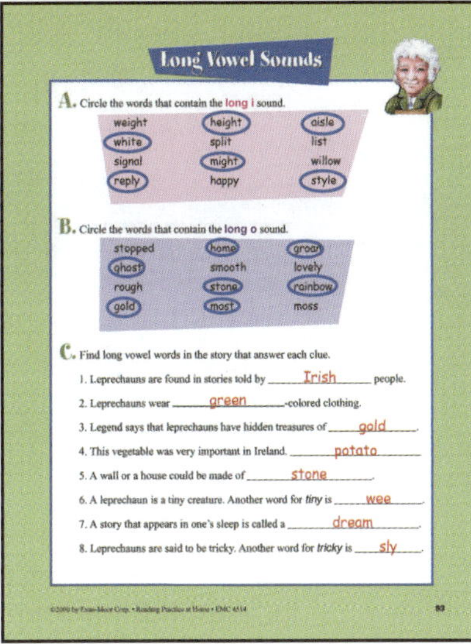

Long Vowel Sounds

A. Circle the words that contain the long i sound.

weight, height, aisle, white, split, list, signal, might, willow, reply, happy, style

B. Circle the words that contain the long o sound.

stopped, home, groan, ghost, smooth, lovely, rough, stone, rainbow, gold, most, moss

C. Find long vowel words in the story that answer each clue.

1. Leprechauns are found in stories told by Irish people.
2. Leprechauns wear green-colored clothing.
3. Legend says that leprechauns have hidden treasures of gold.
4. This vegetable was very important in Ireland. potato
5. A wall or a house could be made of stone.
6. A leprechaun is a tiny creature. Another word for *tiny* is wee.
7. A story that appears in one's sleep is called a dream.
8. Leprechauns are said to be tricky. Another word for *tricky* is sly.

Page 92

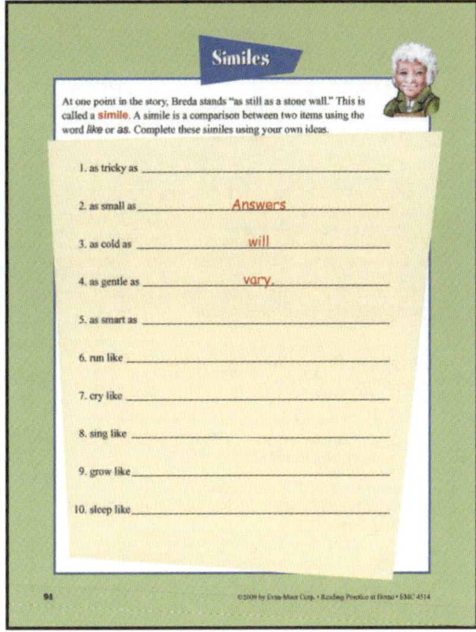

Similes

At one point in the story, Breda stands "as still as a stone wall." This is called a **simile**. A simile is a comparison between two items using the word *like* or *as*. Complete these similes using your own ideas.

1. as tricky as
2. as small as Answers
3. as cold as will
4. as gentle as vary.
5. as smart as
6. run like
7. cry like
8. sing like
9. grow like
10. sleep like

Page 93

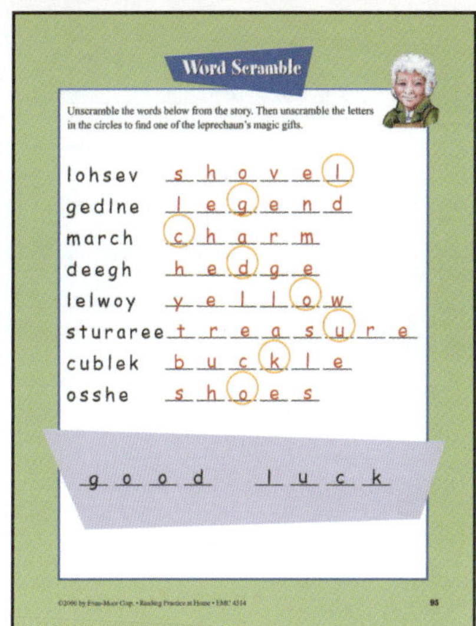

Word Scramble

Unscramble the words below from the story. Then unscramble the letters in the circles to find one of the leprechaun's magic gifts.

lohsev — shovel
gedlne — legend
march — charm
deegh — hedge
lelwoy — yellow
sturaree — treasure
cublek — buckle
osshe — shoes

good luck

Page 97

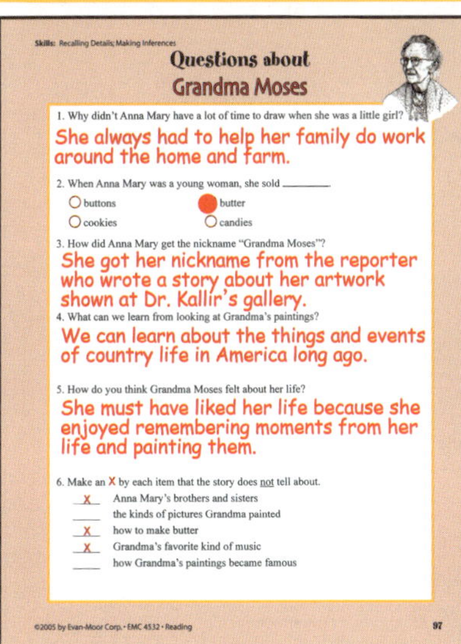

Skills: Recalling Details; Making Inferences

Questions about Grandma Moses

1. Why didn't Anna Mary have a lot of time to draw when she was a little girl?
   She always had to help her family do work around the home and farm.
2. When Anna Mary was a young woman, she sold ______.
   - buttons
   - butter (filled in)
   - cookies
   - candies
3. How did Anna Mary get the nickname "Grandma Moses"?
   She got her nickname from the reporter who wrote a story about her artwork shown at Dr. Kallir's gallery.
4. What can we learn from looking at Grandma's paintings?
   We can learn about the things and events of country life in America long ago.
5. How do you think Grandma Moses felt about her life?
   She must have liked her life because she enjoyed remembering moments from her life and painting them.
6. Make an X by each item that the story does not tell about.
   - X Anna Mary's brothers and sisters
   - the kinds of pictures Grandma painted
   - X how to make butter
   - X Grandma's favorite kind of music
   - how Grandma's paintings became famous

Page 98

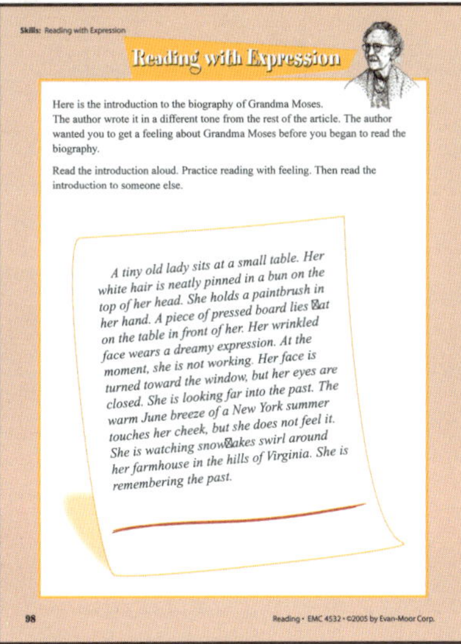

Skills: Reading with Expression

Reading with Expression

Here is the introduction to the biography of Grandma Moses. The author wrote it in a different tone from the rest of the article. The author wanted you to get a feeling about Grandma Moses before you began to read the biography.

Read the introduction aloud. Practice reading with feeling. Then read the introduction to someone else.

A tiny old lady sits at a small table. Her white hair is neatly pinned in a bun on the top of her head. She holds a paintbrush in her hand. A piece of pressed board lies flat on the table in front of her. Her wrinkled face wears a dreamy expression. At the moment, she is not working. Her face is turned toward the window, but her eyes are closed. She is looking far into the past. The warm June breeze of a New York summer touches her cheek, but she does not feel it. She is watching snowflakes swirl around her farmhouse in the hills of Virginia. She is remembering the past.

Page 99

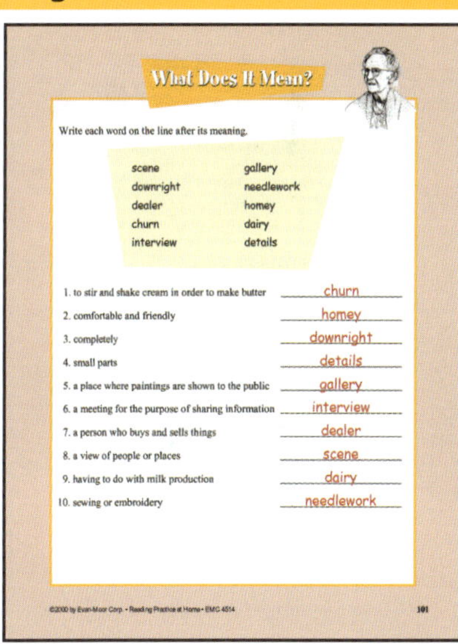

What Does It Mean?

Write each word on the line after its meaning.

scene, gallery, downright, needlework, dealer, homey, churn, dairy, interview, details

1. to stir and shake cream in order to make butter — churn
2. comfortable and friendly — homey
3. completely — downright
4. small parts — details
5. a place where paintings are shown to the public — gallery
6. a meeting for the purpose of sharing information — interview
7. a person who buys and sells things — dealer
8. a view of people or places — scene
9. having to do with milk production — dairy
10. sewing or embroidery — needlework

Page 100

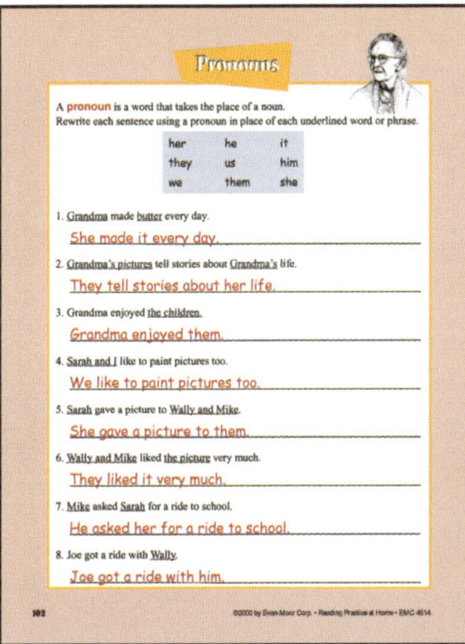

Pronouns

A **pronoun** is a word that takes the place of a noun.
Rewrite each sentence using a pronoun in place of each underlined word or phrase.

her, he, it, they, us, him, we, them, she

1. Grandma made butter every day.
   She made it every day.
2. Grandma's pictures tell stories about Grandma's life.
   They tell stories about her life.
3. Grandma enjoyed the children.
   Grandma enjoyed them.
4. Sarah and I like to paint pictures too.
   We like to paint pictures too.
5. Sarah gave a picture to Wally and Mike.
   She gave a picture to them.
6. Wally and Mike liked the picture very much.
   They liked it very much.
7. Mike asked Sarah for a ride to school.
   He asked her for a ride to school.
8. Joe got a ride with Wally.
   Joe got a ride with him.

Page 101

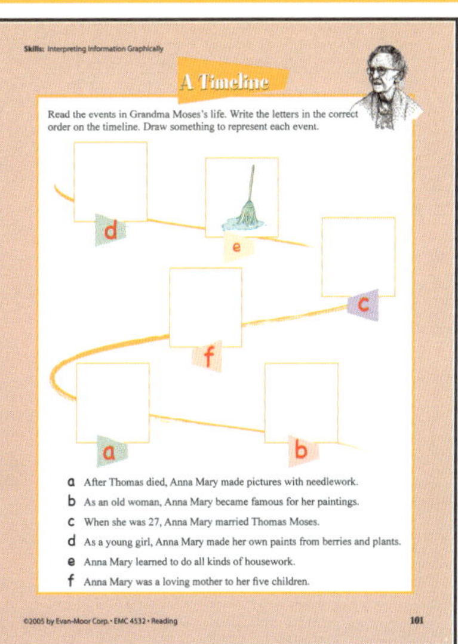

Skills: Interpreting Information Graphically

A Timeline

Read the events in Grandma Moses's life. Write the letters in the correct order on the timeline. Draw something to represent each event.

Timeline order: d, e, c, f, a, b

a. After Thomas died, Anna Mary made pictures with needlework.
b. As an old woman, Anna Mary became famous for her paintings.
c. When she was 27, Anna Mary married Thomas Moses.
d. As a young girl, Anna Mary made her own paints from berries and plants.
e. Anna Mary learned to do all kinds of housework.
f. Anna Mary was a loving mother to her five children.

Page 102

Answers will vary. Possible answers:

Categories

Fill in each category of the chart using words that begin with the letters given.

	colors	animals	plants	foods
r	red, raspberry, rust	rat, rattlesnake, rabbit	rose, ragweed, radish	radish, rhubarb, raisin
p	purple, pink, periwinkle	polar bear, pig, penguin	petunia, pansy, poinsettia	peanut, popcorn, potato
b	black, brown, beige	bear, bat, buffalo	bromeliade, broccoli, begonia	bean, banana, biscuit
g	green, gold, gray	goat, goose, gorilla	grass, geranium, gardenia	grape, goulash, grapefruit

Page 103

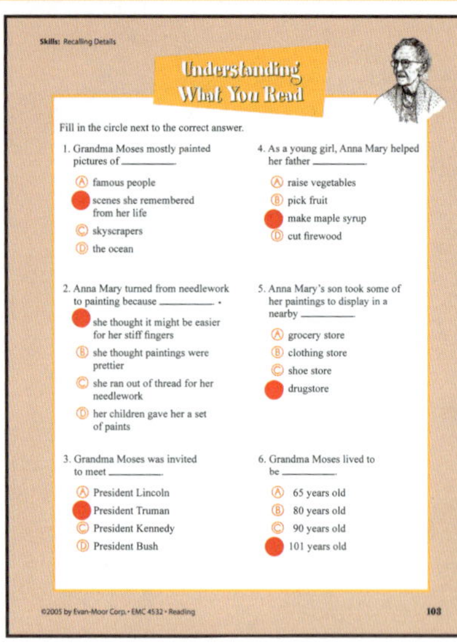

Skills: Recalling Details

Understanding What You Read

Fill in the circle next to the correct answer.

1. Grandma Moses mostly painted pictures of ________.
   - Ⓐ famous people
   - ● scenes she remembered from her life
   - Ⓒ skyscrapers
   - Ⓓ the ocean
2. Anna Mary turned from needlework to painting because ________.
   - ● she thought it might be easier for her stiff fingers
   - Ⓑ she thought paintings were prettier
   - Ⓒ she ran out of thread for her needlework
   - Ⓓ her children gave her a set of paints
3. Grandma Moses was invited to meet ________.
   - Ⓐ President Lincoln
   - ● President Truman
   - Ⓒ President Kennedy
   - Ⓓ President Bush
4. As a young girl, Anna Mary helped her father ________.
   - Ⓐ raise vegetables
   - Ⓑ pick fruit
   - ● make maple syrup
   - Ⓓ cut firewood
5. Anna Mary's son took some of her paintings to display in a nearby ________.
   - Ⓐ grocery store
   - Ⓑ clothing store
   - Ⓒ shoe store
   - ● drugstore
6. Grandma Moses lived to be ________.
   - Ⓐ 65 years old
   - Ⓑ 80 years old
   - Ⓒ 90 years old
   - ● 101 years old

©2005 by Evan-Moor Corp. • EMC 4532 • Reading 103

Page 107

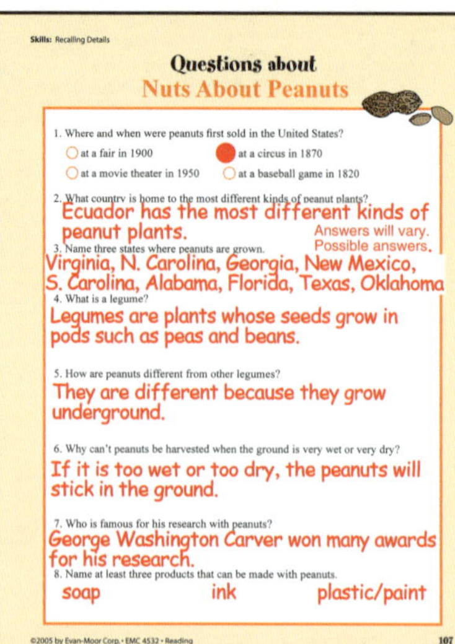

Skills: Recalling Details

Questions about Nuts About Peanuts

1. Where and when were peanuts first sold in the United States?
   - ○ at a fair in 1900
   - ● at a circus in 1870
   - ○ at a movie theater in 1950
   - ○ at a baseball game in 1820
2. What country is home to the most different kinds of peanut plants?
   Ecuador has the most different kinds of peanut plants.
   Answers will vary. Possible answers.
3. Name three states where peanuts are grown.
   Virginia, N. Carolina, Georgia, New Mexico, S. Carolina, Alabama, Florida, Texas, Oklahoma
4. What is a legume?
   Legumes are plants whose seeds grow in pods such as peas and beans.
5. How are peanuts different from other legumes?
   They are different because they grow underground.
6. Why can't peanuts be harvested when the ground is very wet or very dry?
   If it is too wet or too dry, the peanuts will stick in the ground.
7. Who is famous for his research with peanuts?
   George Washington Carver won many awards for his research.
8. Name at least three products that can be made with peanuts.
   soap ink plastic/paint

©2005 by Evan-Moor Corp. • EMC 4532 • Reading 107

Page 108

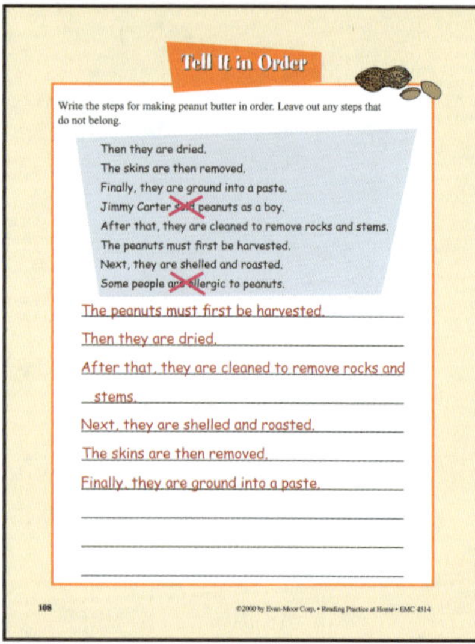

Tell It in Order

Write the steps for making peanut butter in order. Leave out any steps that do not belong.

Then they are dried.
The skins are then removed.
Finally, they are ground into a paste.
Jimmy Carter sold peanuts as a boy.
After that, they are cleaned to remove rocks and stems.
The peanuts must first be harvested.
Next, they are shelled and roasted.
Some people are allergic to peanuts.

The peanuts must first be harvested.
Then they are dried.
After that, they are cleaned to remove rocks and stems.
Next, they are shelled and roasted.
The skins are then removed.
Finally, they are ground into a paste.

108 ©2000 by Evan-Moor Corp. • Reading Practice at Home • EMC 4514

Page 109

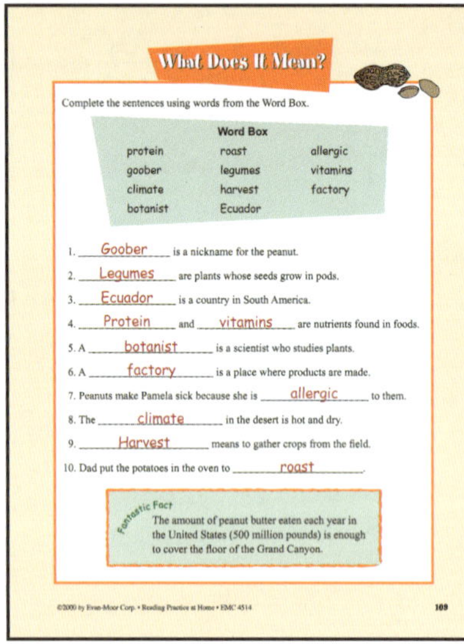

What Does It Mean?

Complete the sentences using words from the Word Box.

Word Box

protein	roast	allergic
goober	legumes	vitamins
climate	harvest	factory
botanist	Ecuador	

1. Goober is a nickname for the peanut.
2. Legumes are plants whose seeds grow in pods.
3. Ecuador is a country in South America.
4. Protein and vitamins are nutrients found in foods.
5. A botanist is a scientist who studies plants.
6. A factory is a place where products are made.
7. Peanuts make Pamela sick because she is allergic to them.
8. The climate in the desert is hot and dry.
9. Harvest means to gather crops from the field.
10. Dad put the potatoes in the oven to roast.

Fantastic Fact: The amount of peanut butter eaten each year in the United States (500 million pounds) is enough to cover the floor of the Grand Canyon.

©2000 by Evan-Moor Corp. • Reading Practice at Home • EMC 4514 109

Page 110

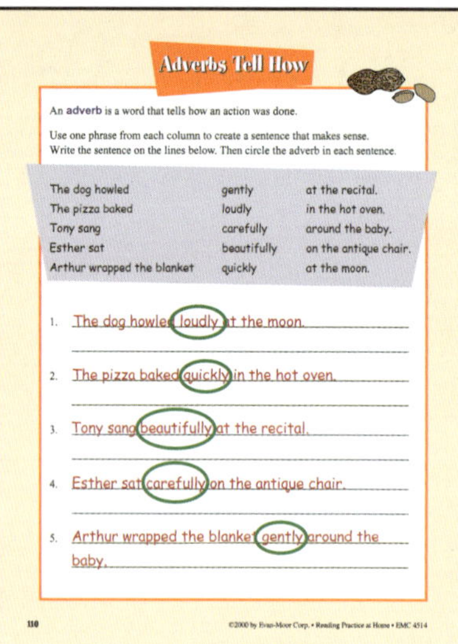

Adverbs Tell How

An adverb is a word that tells how an action was done.

Use one phrase from each column to create a sentence that makes sense. Write the sentence on the lines below. Then circle the adverb in each sentence.

The dog howled	gently	at the recital.
The pizza baked	loudly	in the hot oven.
Tony sang	carefully	around the baby.
Esther sat	beautifully	on the antique chair.
Arthur wrapped the blanket	quickly	at the moon.

1. The dog howled loudly at the moon.
2. The pizza baked quickly in the hot oven.
3. Tony sang beautifully at the recital.
4. Esther sat carefully on the antique chair.
5. Arthur wrapped the blanket gently around the baby.

110 ©2000 by Evan-Moor Corp. • Reading Practice at Home • EMC 4514

Page 111

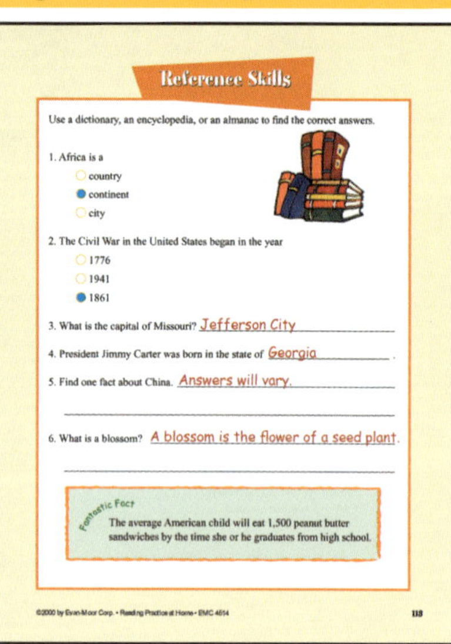

Reference Skills

Use a dictionary, an encyclopedia, or an almanac to find the correct answers.

1. Africa is a
   - ○ country
   - ● continent
   - ○ city
2. The Civil War in the United States began in the year
   - ○ 1776
   - ○ 1941
   - ● 1861
3. What is the capital of Missouri? Jefferson City
4. President Jimmy Carter was born in the state of Georgia.
5. Find one fact about China. Answers will vary.
6. What is a blossom? A blossom is the flower of a seed plant.

Fantastic Fact: The average American child will eat 1,500 peanut butter sandwiches by the time she or he graduates from high school.

©2000 by Evan-Moor Corp. • Reading Practice at Home • EMC 4514 111

Page 112

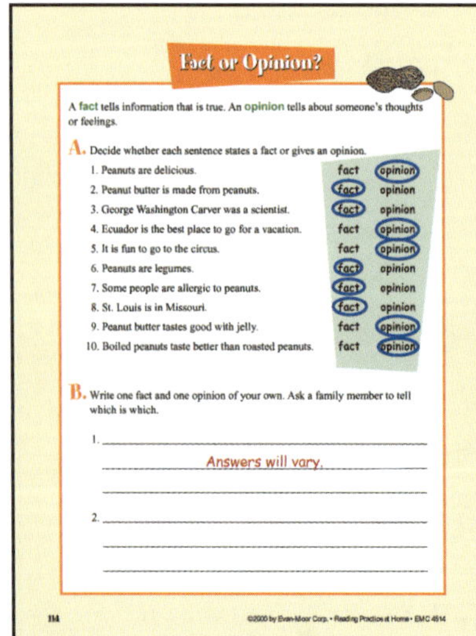

Fact or Opinion?

A fact tells information that is true. An opinion tells about someone's thoughts or feelings.

A. Decide whether each sentence states a fact or gives an opinion.

1. Peanuts are delicious. — opinion
2. Peanut butter is made from peanuts. — fact
3. George Washington Carver was a scientist. — fact
4. Ecuador is the best place to go for a vacation. — opinion
5. It is fun to go to the circus. — opinion
6. Peanuts are legumes. — fact
7. Some people are allergic to peanuts. — fact
8. St. Louis is in Missouri. — fact
9. Peanut butter tastes good with jelly. — opinion
10. Boiled peanuts taste better than roasted peanuts. — opinion

B. Write one fact and one opinion of your own. Ask a family member to tell which is which.

1. Answers will vary.
2.

114 ©2000 by Evan-Moor Corp. • Reading Practice at Home • EMC 4514

Page 116

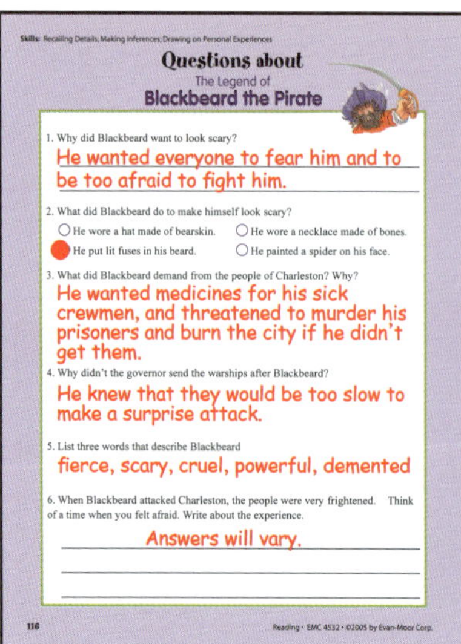

Skills: Recalling Details; Making Inferences; Drawing on Personal Experiences

Questions about The Legend of Blackbeard the Pirate

1. Why did Blackbeard want to look scary?
   He wanted everyone to fear him and to be too afraid to fight him.
2. What did Blackbeard do to make himself look scary?
   - ○ He wore a hat made of bearskin.
   - ○ He wore a necklace made of bones.
   - ● He put lit fuses in his beard.
   - ○ He painted a spider on his face.
3. What did Blackbeard demand from the people of Charleston? Why?
   He wanted medicines for his sick crewmen, and threatened to murder his prisoners and burn the city if he didn't get them.
4. Why didn't the governor send the warships after Blackbeard?
   He knew that they would be too slow to make a surprise attack.
5. List three words that describe Blackbeard.
   fierce, scary, cruel, powerful, demented
6. When Blackbeard attacked Charleston, the people were very frightened. Think of a time when you felt afraid. Write about the experience.
   Answers will vary.

116 Reading • EMC 4532 • ©2005 by Evan-Moor Corp.

Page 117

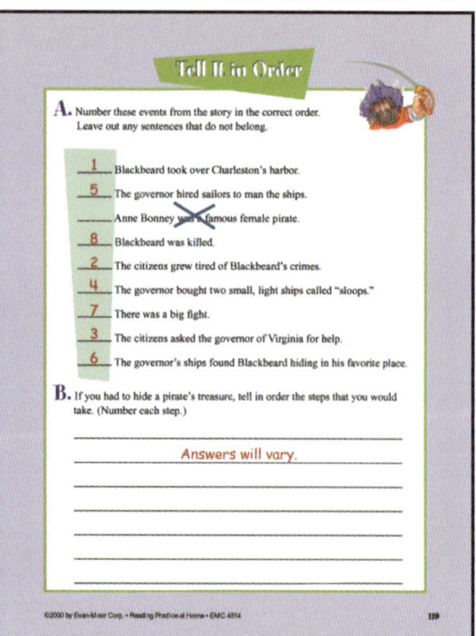

Tell It in Order

A. Number these events from the story in the correct order. Leave out any sentences that do not belong.

- 1 Blackbeard took over Charleston's harbor.
- 5 The governor hired sailors to man the ships.
- Anne Bonney was a famous female pirate.
- 8 Blackbeard was killed.
- 2 The citizens grew tired of Blackbeard's crimes.
- 4 The governor bought two small, light ships called "sloops."
- 7 There was a big fight.
- 3 The citizens asked the governor of Virginia for help.
- 6 The governor's ships found Blackbeard hiding in his favorite place.

B. If you had to hide a pirate's treasure, tell in order the steps that you would take. (Number each step.)

Answers will vary.

©2000 by Evan-Moor Corp. • Reading Practice at Home • EMC 4514 119

Page 118

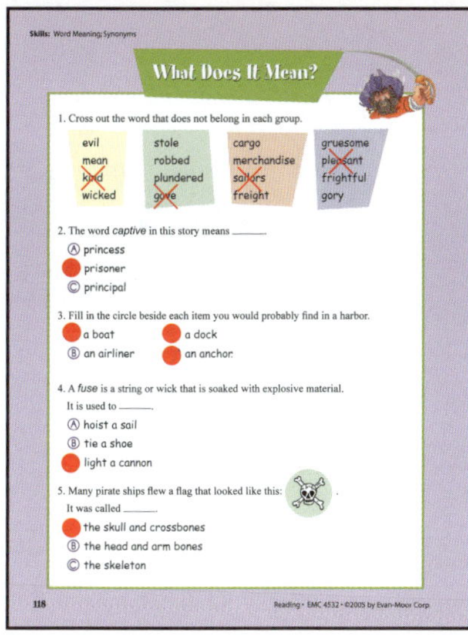

Skills: Word Meaning; Synonyms

What Does It Mean?

1. Cross out the word that does not belong in each group.

evil	stole	cargo	gruesome
mean	robbed	merchandise	~~pleasant~~
~~kind~~	plundered	~~sailors~~	frightful
wicked	~~gave~~	freight	gory

2. The word *captive* in this story means ____.
   Ⓐ princess
   ● prisoner
   Ⓒ principal

3. Fill in the circle beside each item you would probably find in a harbor.
   ● a boat
   ● a dock
   Ⓑ an airliner
   ● an anchor

4. A *fuse* is a string or wick that is soaked with explosive material. It is used to ____.
   Ⓐ hoist a sail
   Ⓑ tie a shoe
   ● light a cannon

5. Many pirate ships flew a flag that looked like this: It was called ____.
   ● the skull and crossbones
   Ⓑ the head and arm bones
   Ⓒ the skeleton

118 Reading • EMC 4532 • ©2005 by Evan-Moor Corp.

Page 119

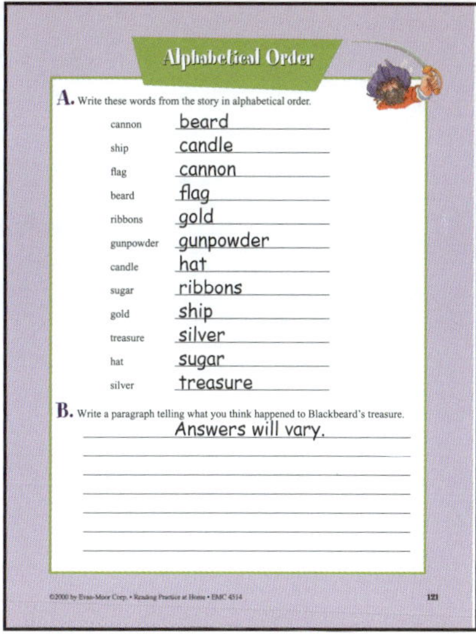

Alphabetical Order

A. Write these words from the story in alphabetical order.

cannon	beard
ship	candle
flag	cannon
beard	flag
ribbons	gold
gunpowder	gunpowder
candle	hat
sugar	ribbons
gold	ship
treasure	silver
hat	sugar
silver	treasure

B. Write a paragraph telling what you think happened to Blackbeard's treasure.

Answers will vary.

©2000 by Evan-Moor Corp. • Reading Practice at Home • EMC 4514 121

Page 120

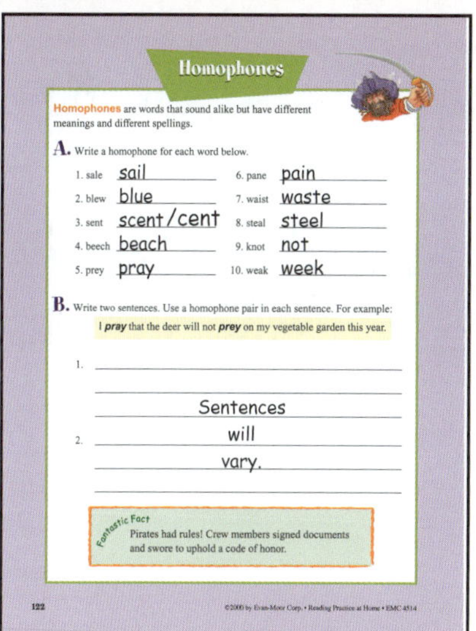

Homophones

Homophones are words that sound alike but have different meanings and different spellings.

A. Write a homophone for each word below.

1. sale sail
2. blew blue
3. sent scent/cent
4. beech beach
5. prey pray
6. pane pain
7. waist waste
8. steal steel
9. knot not
10. weak week

B. Write two sentences. Use a homophone pair in each sentence. For example:

I *pray* that the deer will not *prey* on my vegetable garden this year.

1.
2.

Sentences will vary.

Fantastic Fact: Pirates had rules! Crew members signed documents and swore to uphold a code of honor.

122 ©2000 by Evan-Moor Corp. • Reading Practice at Home • EMC 4514

Page 121

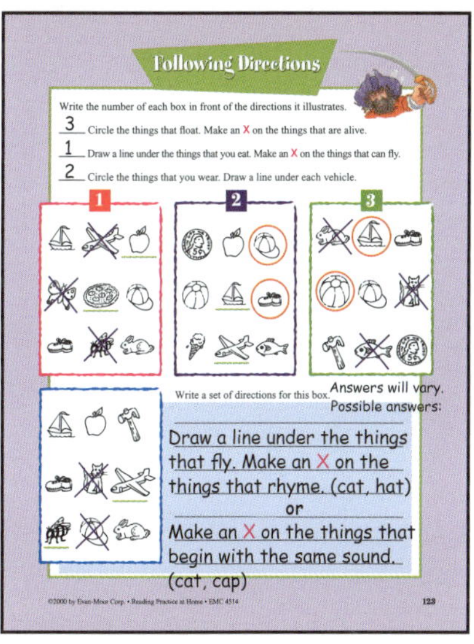

Following Directions

Write the number of each box in front of the directions it illustrates.

3 Circle the things that float. Make an X on the things that are alive.

1 Draw a line under the things that you eat. Make an X on the things that can fly.

2 Circle the things that you wear. Draw a line under each vehicle.

Write a set of directions for this box.

Answers will vary. Possible answers:

Draw a line under the things that fly. Make an X on the things that rhyme. (cat, hat)

or

Make an X on the things that begin with the same sound. (cat, cap)

©2000 by Evan-Moor Corp. • Reading Practice at Home • EMC 4514 123

Page 123

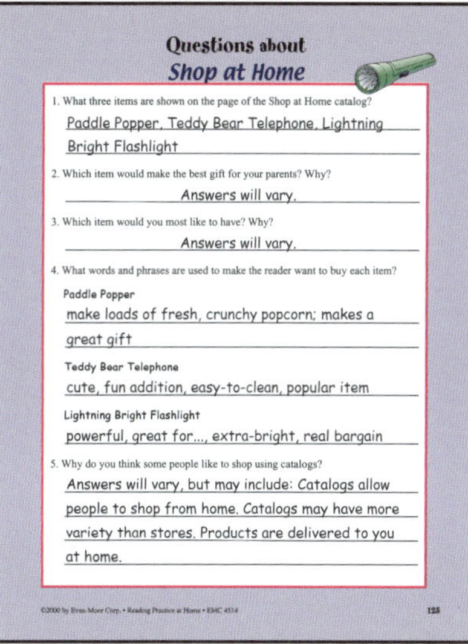

Questions about *Shop at Home*

1. What three items are shown on the page of the Shop at Home catalog?
   Paddle Popper, Teddy Bear Telephone, Lightning Bright Flashlight
2. Which item would make the best gift for your parents? Why?
   Answers will vary.
3. Which item would you most like to have? Why?
   Answers will vary.
4. What words and phrases are used to make the reader want to buy each item?
   Paddle Popper: make loads of fresh, crunchy popcorn; makes a great gift
   Teddy Bear Telephone: cute, fun addition, easy-to-clean, popular item
   Lightning Bright Flashlight: powerful, great for..., extra-bright, real bargain
5. Why do you think some people like to shop using catalogs?
   Answers will vary, but may include: Catalogs allow people to shop from home. Catalogs may have more variety than stores. Products are delivered to you at home.

©2000 by Evan-Moor Corp. • Reading Practice at Home • EMC 4514 125

Page 124

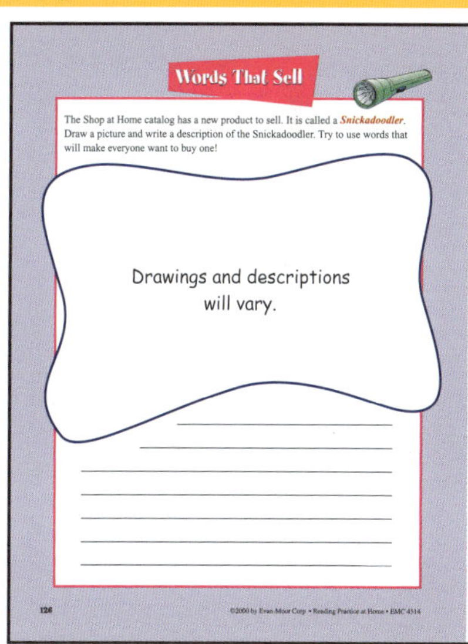

Words That Sell

The Shop at Home catalog has a new product to sell. It is called a *Snickadoodler*. Draw a picture and write a description of the Snickadoodler. Try to use words that will make everyone want to buy one!

Drawings and descriptions will vary.

126 ©2000 by Evan-Moor Corp. • Reading Practice at Home • EMC 4514

Page 128

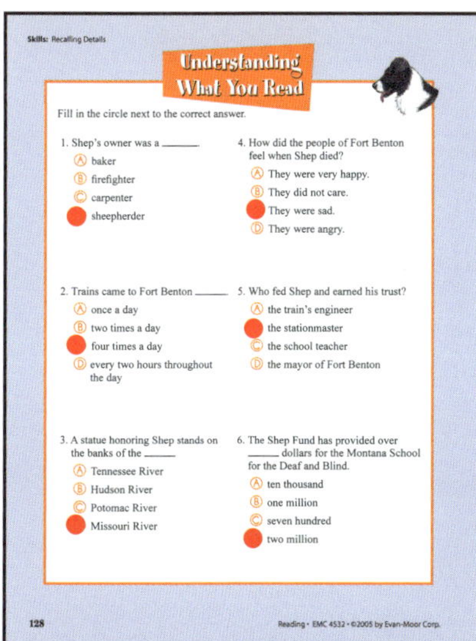

Skills: Recalling Details

Understanding What You Read

Fill in the circle next to the correct answer.

1. Shep's owner was a ____.
   Ⓐ baker
   Ⓑ firefighter
   Ⓒ carpenter
   ● sheepherder
2. Trains came to Fort Benton ____.
   Ⓐ once a day
   Ⓑ two times a day
   ● four times a day
   Ⓓ every two hours throughout the day
3. A statue honoring Shep stands on the banks of the ____.
   Ⓐ Tennessee River
   Ⓑ Hudson River
   Ⓒ Potomac River
   ● Missouri River
4. How did the people of Fort Benton feel when Shep died?
   Ⓐ They were very happy.
   Ⓑ They did not care.
   ● They were sad.
   Ⓓ They were angry.
5. Who fed Shep and earned his trust?
   Ⓐ the train's engineer
   ● the stationmaster
   Ⓒ the school teacher
   Ⓓ the mayor of Fort Benton
6. The Shep Fund has provided over ____ dollars for the Montana School for the Deaf and Blind.
   Ⓐ ten thousand
   Ⓑ one million
   Ⓒ seven hundred
   ● two million

128 Reading • EMC 4532 • ©2005 by Evan-Moor Corp.

Page 129

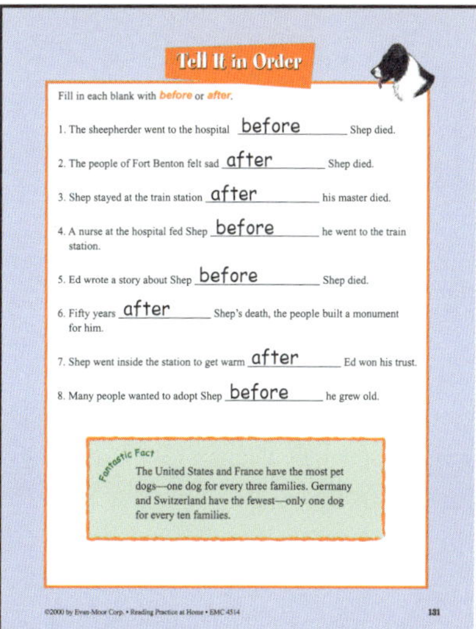

Tell It in Order

Fill in each blank with *before* or *after*.

1. The sheepherder went to the hospital before Shep died.
2. The people of Fort Benton felt sad after Shep died.
3. Shep stayed at the train station after his master died.
4. A nurse at the hospital fed Shep before he went to the train station.
5. Ed wrote a story about Shep before Shep died.
6. Fifty years after Shep's death, the people built a monument for him.
7. Shep went inside the station to get warm after Ed won his trust.
8. Many people wanted to adopt Shep before he grew old.

Fantastic Fact: The United States and France have the most pet dogs—one dog for every three families. Germany and Switzerland have the fewest—only one dog for every ten families.

©2000 by Evan-Moor Corp. • Reading Practice at Home • EMC 4514 131

Page 130

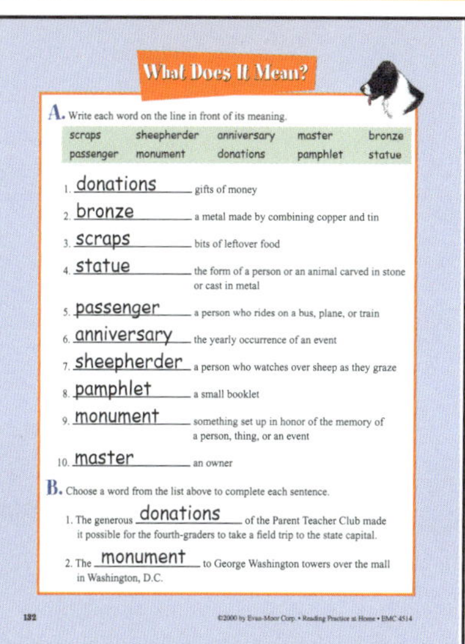

What Does It Mean?

A. Write each word on the line in front of its meaning.

scraps	sheepherder	anniversary	master	bronze
passenger	monument	donations	pamphlet	statue

1. donations — gifts of money
2. bronze — a metal made by combining copper and tin
3. scraps — bits of leftover food
4. statue — the form of a person or an animal carved in stone or cast in metal
5. passenger — a person who rides on a bus, plane, or train
6. anniversary — the yearly occurrence of an event
7. sheepherder — a person who watches over sheep as they graze
8. pamphlet — a small booklet
9. monument — something set up in honor of the memory of a person, thing, or an event
10. master — an owner

B. Choose a word from the list above to complete each sentence.

1. The generous donations of the Parent Teacher Club made it possible for the fourth-graders to take a field trip to the state capital.
2. The monument to George Washington towers over the mall in Washington, D.C.

132 ©2000 by Evan-Moor Corp. • Reading Practice at Home • EMC 4514

Page 131

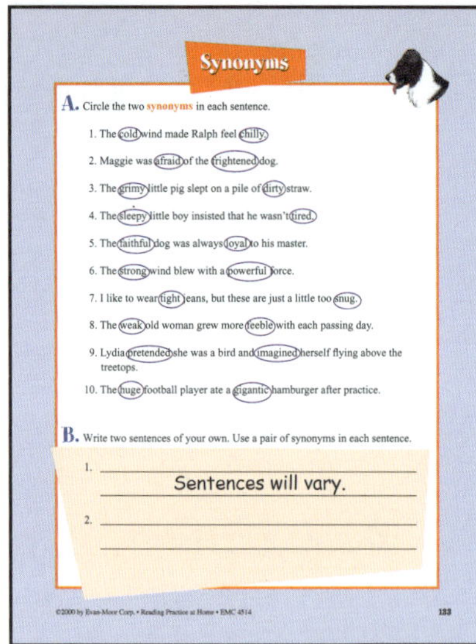

Synonyms

A. Circle the two **synonyms** in each sentence.

1. The (cold) wind made Ralph feel (chilly).
2. Maggie was (afraid) of the (frightened) dog.
3. The (grimy) little pig slept on a pile of (dirty) straw.
4. The (sleepy) little boy insisted that he wasn't (tired).
5. The (faithful) dog was always (loyal) to his master.
6. The (strong) wind blew with a (powerful) force.
7. I like to wear (tight) jeans, but these are just a little too (snug).
8. The (weak) old woman grew more (feeble) with each passing day.
9. Lydia (pretended) she was a bird and (imagined) herself flying above the treetops.
10. The (huge) football player ate a (gigantic) hamburger after practice.

B. Write two sentences of your own. Use a pair of synonyms in each sentence.

1. Sentences will vary.
2.

©2000 by Evan-Moor Corp. • Reading Practice at Home • EMC 4514

Page 132

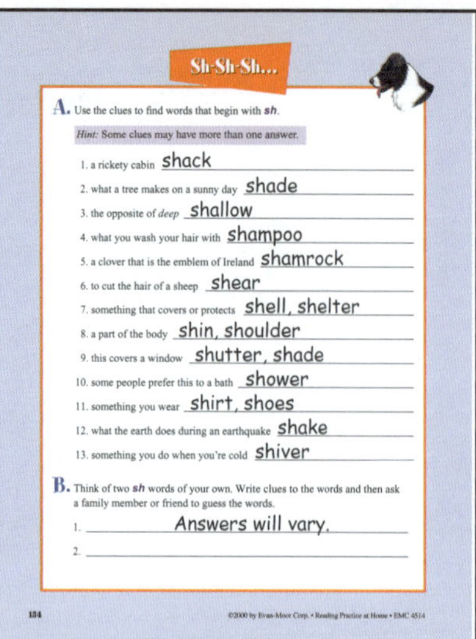

Sh-Sh-Sh...

A. Use the clues to find words that begin with ***sh***.

Hint: Some clues may have more than one answer.

1. a rickety cabin — shack
2. what a tree makes on a sunny day — shade
3. the opposite of *deep* — shallow
4. what you wash your hair with — shampoo
5. a clover that is the emblem of Ireland — shamrock
6. to cut the hair of a sheep — shear
7. something that covers or protects — shell, shelter
8. a part of the body — shin, shoulder
9. this covers a window — shutter, shade
10. some people prefer this to a bath — shower
11. something you wear — shirt, shoes
12. what the earth does during an earthquake — shake
13. something you do when you're cold — shiver

B. Think of two ***sh*** words of your own. Write clues to the words and then ask a family member or friend to guess the words.

1. Answers will vary.
2.

©2000 by Evan-Moor Corp. • Reading Practice at Home • EMC 4514